HOW TO WRITE A PLAY
for the Amateur Stage

D1102989

Other Allison & Busby 'Writers' Guides'

HOW TO WRITE A PLAY

for the Amateur Stage

Dilys Gater

ALLISON & BUSBY

To Pamela Shufflebotham and Norman Williams

The author would like to acknowledge the assistance of
the following during the writing of this book:

Amanda Smith at Samuel French's London office, Peggy
Poole and Anne Warr in the Wirral, Graham Humphreys
and his play (as yet unwritten) about Charles going
bankrupt.

An Allison & Busby book
Published in 1990 by
W. H. Allen & Co. Plc
Unit 26, Grand Union Centre,
338 Ladbroke Grove,
London W10 5AH

Phototypeset by Input Typesetting Ltd, London
Printed in Great Britain by
Cox & Wyman Ltd, Reading, Berks.

ISBN 0 74900 090 2

Contents

INTRODUCTION

So you want to write a play; you're longing to get this play of yours down on paper but you'd like a bit of help as to how to go about it.

Maybe you act with an Amateur Dramatic Society and you've thought of an idea that seems as if it would make a good stage play; possibly you've never acted at all, but writing a play appeals to you more than writing articles or a novel; you want to write something for your Youth Group, your W.I. group or the dedicated seven of you who make up your local Stanislavsky Society to perform; or you're desperate to find a script that takes into account the fact that, though your company is keen, it consists of two men, fifteen women, a cat and a parrot, and you can't possibly leave anybody out; perhaps, worst of all, you've been persuaded by subtle blackmail to come up with a text that can be entered in the Original Play Section of your local Drama Festival next year by your enthusiastic producer who's too busy to sit down and do it herself. Or you simply cherish a dream of seeing your own characters come to life on the stage, speaking lines you've written.

Whatever the reason, this book is for you, as you scratch your head and wonder just how to get started. It isn't for geniuses who want to create their own rules, or innovators who want to alter the whole concept of Twentieth Century

Drama, or for professional playwrights with long lists of successful plays behind them – it's for anyone with the modest ambition of writing a good play that an amateur group will enjoy performing.

Interested? Then read on. . . .

Chapter One

WHAT IS A PLAY?

A play is a dream, an inspiration, somebody's brain-child which comes to brief, dazzling life when the talents of actors and actresses, producer, stage crew, designer, are added and, in the glare of the lights, it takes to the boards before an audience, that faceless mass which will laugh, cry, applaud or hiss, in what is essentially a vital and shared experience. As the author, the Playwright, you may be called upon to join in the glitter and the glamour of those ecstatic First Night curtain calls, to smile and bow as the cast joins with the audience in appreciation of your work, but basically, your place is not on the stage but in some little corner alone with your typewriter, or pen and papers. Long before the curtain rises, you will have written your play, moved on to other things. For what you write will be in the nature of a blueprint, a guide, a record to assist others in the successful translation of your ideas to a three-dimensional form.

For the playwright, writing a play is by no means a glamorous business. It's a skilled job, which you have to wrestle with alone. Think of a bridge-builder who draws the plans for a wonderful new bridge. In his office, he juggles with set-squares and rulers, formulae that will ensure the bridge will look fragile and graceful, but will be capable of carrying heavy traffic. He does all the thinking, the working out, long before the day when, to the strains of a band, the

1

newly-built bridge is declared open and the press are there to take pictures.

You too will be building a bridge, a plan to indicate to producers, actors and actresses how you want them to interpret your ideas on the stage. And so you record all the details they will need to know – what scenery is necessary, what the characters say, what they do. Unlike a novel or a short story, a play, though complete in itself, is not the finished product, and you should bear in mind all the time you are writing that this is strictly business, everything you put down is there for a purpose, and must be clear and workable, with no ramblings off into long-winded explanations or your own random thoughts, or effusive descriptions.

In a play, the author keeps himself or herself very much in the background. You write directions, you put speeches into the mouths of your characters, but your own voice should ideally never be heard. You are the schemer, the planner, the builder, the moving force behind the great event, but on the night your play is performed, the greatest tribute audiences will ever pay you is to forget, in their delight and pleasure at the moving experience they have just lived through, that there was actually an author at all.

Setting out your script

A novel in its final form appears on the shelves of bookshops neatly bound with an arresting cover. Your play, as you will present it to your company or to any other interested parties, will consist of clearly-typed pages of manuscript, your own personal file of instructions to the players.

Because it consists mainly of lines of dialogue, interspersed with stage directions, a play-script is set out differently to a novel or a story. There are no paragraphs in a play-script, no chapters.

Type on A4 paper in double spacing, making sure you

2

keep a clean and accurate copy. Leave reasonable 1" margins on both sides. Number each page clearly and consecutively throughout the play, never by Act or Scene.

A one-act play, lasting about half-an-hour, will consist of 16–20 pages, and ideally will not be split into scenes, so you just carry straight on to the end. A full-length play will consist of about 70 pages and will need to be divided into Acts, maybe with Scenes within each Act. Traditionally, full-length plays consist of three Acts, but since nowadays there is usually only one interval, you may prefer to split your play into two Acts. Generally, the First Act is the longest, and if you are going to have two, the Second Act will be slightly shorter.

If you intend to keep to the traditional three Acts, the First Act is still the longest, with the second slightly shorter, and the third shortest of all. Each Act should start on a fresh sheet of paper, and if you have two Scenes within an Act, you can also start each Scene on a fresh sheet. Make sure you mark each Act or Scene clearly, i.e. at the top of the page ACT ONE or ACT TWO, SCENE TWO.

Your script will start with a cover page on which you put the title of the play, and any other information such as *A One-Act Play* or *The Story of Mary, Queen of Scots,* followed by your name (or pseudonym). Since many people often borrow scripts to consider or read, saying they will return them and neglecting to do so, it's as well to be sure your address and phone number are clearly visible on this cover page as well as on any covering letters you might write if you send a script through the post, then nobody will be able to say innocently: 'But there was no address, so I didn't know how to get it back to you.'

Following your cover page is a separate sheet of paper with a list of the characters who appear in the play, an explanation of where the play takes place, and the period in which it is set.

At one time it was fashionable to describe each character in great detail, including their age, hair colour and what

3

clothes they were wearing, but this is no longer necessary, since even if you are writing for your own group, physical characteristics and colours of clothes will be dictated by what is available. So leave such minutiae to the Wardrobe Mistress, the designer and the producer. Remember, you're only laying out the plan, the blueprint, and you must be prepared to let others contribute their own specialised knowledge to what has to be, in the final analysis, a team effort. All you need to add to the names of the characters is anything relevant to the plot, such as the relationship one character may have with another, e.g. MONICA GOLD (James's sister).

After your list of characters you state the SCENE, and give it briefly. In a one-act play, there should only be one SCENE, so your entry here may run something like:

> **SCENE:** The Rev. Ashby's Study in the Rectory, Little Brockleton.

or,

> **SCENE:** A rocky hillside.

When you begin the play, you will naturally explain the setting in a little more detail, but you need only give one sentence here, and the same goes for your last note on TIME. You will need to say the year (roughly) in which the play is set and if necessary and relevant, the time of day and season. Possibly your note might run:

> **TIME:** A winter afternoon, the present.

or

> **TIME:** Paris, 1880.

Note that for a full-length play, where you may have a change of scene between Act One and Act Two, as well as a difference in the time when each Act occurs, you list all the Acts, including all the Scenes if there are variations, and incorporate the time when they take place. Thus your

4

notes for a full-length play, after you have listed the characters, might run:

ACT ONE: The Rev. Ashby's Study in the Rectory, Little Brockleton. A winter afternoon, the present.
ACT TWO: The same, early the next morning.
ACT THREE: The Village Hall, three weeks later.

When your interested reader has perused this page, which gives all the details about who is in your play, where and when it is set, he or she will next turn over to Page 1 of the actual script itself. As I have said, a play-script consists of dialogue for the characters to speak, interspersed where necessary with stage directions. All these must be kept as practical as possible. Comments such as 'Mary, realising she has been fooled and that none of what George told her was true, flushes and raises her head with the self-possession of a duchess' has no place in a play. Your character of Mary should have all this in her one line, which might read simply:

MARY: (after a pause) So you lied to me, George?

The playwright *never* explains. Whether Mary does actually flush and raise her head like a duchess will depend on the actress who will bring her to life on the stage, and the producer who will be interpreting your script. That is their job, so leave it to them; it's what they are there for.

In dialogue, every speech must begin with a new line of type, with the name of the character who is to say it at the beginning in capital letters, underlined if you wish for extra emphasis. The character's name comes close to the left-hand margin, the speech may run on or be kept on the right-hand part of your page. Stage directions can either be centred in the middle of the page (never close to the left margin) or kept with the rest of the text on the right. Some people like to type all their stage directions in capital letters; others find it easier to put them in brackets. Whichever way

5

you choose to do them, you must always write the name of a character, when it appears in stage directions, in capital letters, preferably underlined.

It is sometimes recommended that everything that is not actually intended to be spoken should be underlined in red, but so long as your pages are clear and the stage directions can be picked out easily from the lines of dialogue, there is no real need to do this. Actors and actresses will mark and underline their copies of the script as they work on it during rehearsals, so don't overload your original with heavy underscoring. Keep it clear, keep it easy to read and to follow, those are the main rules.

You should note that printed scripts make use of italics, heavy type and various other things which are beyond the scope of the average typist, so don't worry because the printed book of a play is different to your manuscript. Set your work out in the way that seems easiest and clearest to you, and causes you the least trouble.

The Anatomy of a Stage

It is not necessary for you to be familiar with the complete vocabulary or 'jargon' of the theatre in order to write a play, but in view of the fact that your blueprint has been written specifically to indicate how you want your ideas to be transferred into the medium of a stage performance, there are certain technical terms which may assist you to explain more clearly what you want to say. Also, of course, you need to have at least a basic concept of the different parts which make up the stage where your play will be acted, or you will be labouring under a severe and quite unnecessary handicap.

Whether your play is to be performed in a theatre, a church, a hall, the centre of a large room or out of doors, you refer to the space where the players will perform as the

ACTING AREA. The place or places where the audience will sit or stand is called the AUDITORIUM.

The most familiar way of presenting a play today is with the actors on a raised stage separated from the audience and a wall (real or imaginary) between them. The 'frame' or opening through which the audience watches the play is called the PROSCENIUM. The part of the stage in front of the proscenium, which juts forward into the auditorium, is called the APRON.

The part of the stage the audience can see, where the actors act out the play, you describe as ONSTAGE. The areas at the side and behind it where the production team and stage crew work, which the audience cannot see, is called OFF or OFFSTAGE.

At the front, shutting off or revealing what lies behind the proscenium arch, is the CURTAIN (also sometimes known as the TABS, the FOOTLIGHTS, the FLOATS or the FOURTH WALL). On either side of the stage, there are curtains which hide the offstage area from the view of the audience. These are known as DRAPES or LEGS and usually have openings for players to enter or leave the stage. At the back is the CYC or CYCLORAMA, a plain hanging cloth that covers the back of the stage and can be lit to create an effect of distance or space. Alternatively, the back of the stage may be hidden by a BACKCLOTH or BACKDROP, a large hanging piece of canvas with a scene painted on it. Sometimes a similar cloth is used towards the front of the stage to hide scene changes taking place behind it, while the action continues in front. This is called a FRONTCLOTH.

If you want to set your play simply with plain curtains on all sides, you call this a CURTAIN SET. If the setting is to be more realistic, to represent, say, a room with doors and windows, it is known technically as a BOX SET and will be made up of large pieces of scenery called FLATS. On such a set, the actors and actresses will enter and exit through a door rather than simply leaving the stage through openings in the drapes.

When writing for the stage, all directions for LEFT and RIGHT (i.e. if you want to say that a character must move to the left or right, or if a piece of furniture is placed on the stage on the left or the right) are *always* given from the point of view of the actors facing the audience, not from that of the person in the auditorium watching the stage. Traditionally, LEFT or STAGE LEFT is called the PROMPT SIDE, while STAGE RIGHT is referred to as O.P. (OPPOSITE PROMPT).

If you want to specify 'towards the front of the stage', you use the direction DOWNSTAGE. 'Towards the back of the stage' is referred to as UP or UPSTAGE. CENTRE is of course the central section of the stage. These sections of the stage should be kept in mind as you work out roughly how you want your play to look and what you would like the actors to do, when you are writing the script, though it is not necessary to give directions about movement unless this is essential. The producer will BLOCK or plan all the moves, and the actors will develop things for the characters to do (which they call BUSINESS) when the play is in rehearsal. All the playwright really needs in his blueprint is the words the characters speak and any absolutely essential direction to assist the producer, otherwise, though naturally he will have some idea of his own in mind as to how he thinks the play will work on a stage, he should leave all the headaches of working out the moves for the producer to worry about.

When a stage is made ready for a scene to begin, with all furniture etc in place, this is called SETTING or SETTING THE STAGE. When scenery or props are removed, this is called STRIKING.

And, you will be happy to know, there is more than enough 'jargon' there to make you perfectly competent at writing a play and knowing exactly how this will work when it leaps off the page and onto the stage.

There are, however, a few other useful terms which may help you as you write your play down:

AD LIB – this means, anything the actors say which is not in the script. You can use it as an instruction if you want a crowd of people to mutter or shout, or leave them free to invent their own lines, e.g. 'The crowd surrounds QUEEN ELIZABETH shouting ad lib.'

BLACKOUT – All stage lights go out as well as those in the auditorium (which are already out while the play is on). You can often use a BLACKOUT effectively at the end of an Act or Scene, especially if it follows immediately on a 'surprise' for the audience and you want to end the Scene quickly before they get their breath back, as it were.

CUE – a signal for some sort of activity during a performance. Actors call the lines spoken before they enter, or have to speak themselves, their 'cues'. Certain lines or actions in the play will also provide cues for changes in lighting, sound, effects or work to be done by the stage management team.

DIM or FADE – to reduce the brightness of the lighting on the stage. When the lights DIM or FADE to a BLACKOUT, they go out gradually as opposed to being switched off suddenly.

HOUSE – This refers to the auditorium, and sometimes to the audience as well.

HOUSE LIGHTS – The lights in the auditorium which go out during a performance, but are on before and after the play, and during the intervals.

WINGS – The areas on each side of the stage which cannot be seen by the audience.

From Page to Stage

I cannot emphasise too strongly how practical your script has got to be in every respect, for although someone may write a play that is wonderful on paper, it's no real use if it is impossible to mount in the theatre, hall, room or wherever it is going to be presented. Always bear in mind the confines of a stage, and the fact that your play may be performed by more than one group, in a variety of different venues, which means it has to be easily adapted to a large stage with all mod. cons. or a simple floor space with the audience sitting round the acting area on easy chairs.

It is a sensible idea to try and be as economical and as undemanding as possible with regard to, say, your exits and entrances and any necessary props relevant to the action. You can reasonably suppose that there will be an entrance on each side of the stage, but it would be ridiculous to insist on having three doors and a staircase in your set, when your characters could just as easily all enter through the same door. And though there are celebrated examples of lorries, buses, trapezes, and coaches pulled by teams of horses being introduced onto the stage, I need hardly point out that by including something like this as an essential part of your play, you will only be making things difficult for yourself. Try to keep your set as simple as possible. You want your company (or some company, at any rate) to bring it to life on the stage, so it must be stage-worthy and actable.

There are some playwrights – whether they have theatre experience or not – who insist on being present at all rehearsals of plays they have written, and not only drive producers mad by refusing to agree that it's really not necessary to have pouring rain onstage during the tropical storm scene, or that it will be easier to have a 'fake' snow-man rather than one that actually melts before our eyes (both of which are impossible demands to make on amateur companies) but also take on the task of personally supervising every nuance and inflection that is put into their dialogue by the performers. Needless to say, they are not popular with the companies who might perform their work and quite rightly, since once again, we are up against the fact that the end product, the performance of a play on the stage, is essentially a team effort which needs all the talents and expertise of the other members of the team as well as the playwright who comes up with the script.

Your job stops when you finish work on the last page of your neatly-typed manuscript, unless you are writing a one-man or one-woman show, and producing and acting it yourself. But though you need to keep your end up a bit if you *are* invited to rehearsals and the members of the cast throw Prima Donna fits of temperament, declaring insultingly that: 'These lines are impossible to speak – it's no wonder I keep getting them wrong!' (which can happen, so be prepared – your work may not always be recognised for what it is) you will be foolish if you imagine that only you know exactly how every word should be spoken and exactly how every character will act and react. If you insist that you personally have to specify every item that appears on the stage, choose the colours of the paper flowers that will stand in the vases, loom behind the producer during casting, arguing that SYLVIA has got to be slim and dark, he can't possibly give the part to a plump blonde, you are not only denying the theatrical gifts of others but 'hogging the limelight' in the worst sense.

Once a play gets into rehearsal, it takes on a life of its own, and movements that seemed obvious, for instance, when you were writing the script, will not work; the actors and actresses will develop their own personal gestures and mannerisms as they feel their way into the part without instruction from you; 'business' you might have included (like one of the characters rolling a cigarette) will have to be altered. It isn't easy for an author to stand quietly by and watch what seems like a certain course being set for disaster and the ruin of his precious play, but amazing though it may seem, your script will not only stand, but positively benefit from what seems to you like the producer's point-blank refusal to see exactly what you were getting at.

On one occasion, I wrote a play for a W.I. group about Anne Boleyn's last day in the Tower of London. I saw my character of ANNE very clearly – slim, quick, Frenchified, elegant, sophisticated – so I wrote all her dialogue and stage directions accordingly. When the play was in rehearsal, I went along to see what the producer was getting up to and discovered to my secret horror that the girl who was playing my 'Anne' was a rather stocky, slow-moving 'jolly hockey-sticks' type rather than the beautiful doomed queen I had envisaged. And yet, in spite of my forebodings, this very different interpretation of what I had seen as having only one possible method of being played rose to tremendously powerful heights, won every prize and staggered me with a picture of a regal and convincing 'Anne' I had never in my wildest dreams imagined. It also taught me a humbling and valuable lesson. It's the playwright's job to write the play, get it down on paper, and then let the rest of the team take it from the page to the stage. Don't try to do it all yourself. The producer and the actresses and actors know their jobs better than you do, even if it *is* your play.

Naturally, you want to indicate in your blueprint how you think the play should appear and sound, to your satisfaction, and you might insert bracketed instructions as to how the lines need to be spoken. This is not strictly necessary, and some playwrights never do it, they give just the words. If you were writing for radio or televison, you would probably find that any directions of this sort should be avoided at all costs, but for the stage you have a certain amount of free-dom and can include instructions to the actors, reference to where pauses must occur, or any other details you feel you would like to incorporate. But do not insist these must be followed to the letter, or take offence if the producer decides to ignore them.

Even the bridge-builder probably had his beautifully detailed plans adapted by the construction company who went out in hard hats and actually did the work of putting the rivets in and fitting the pieces of steel girder into place.

Chapter Two

BASIC TECHNIQUES

A lot of the work involved in writing a play has to be done in your head before you go anywhere near your typewriter or sit down and pick up your pen with a purposeful air. The more plays you write, the more you will become familiar with certain basic techniques that will help your play to be a good one.

I'd like to tell you about my own first attempt at writing a play. I was aged about ten, and had spent a childhood appearing in Nativity Plays put on each year by the Sunday School I attended. I don't think I had ever seen a 'real' play. My family lived in a small village and we had no money to spare for trips to the theatre, even if there had been one within reaching distance, so all my experience lay with what the Sunday School, under its very well-meaning but untutored teachers, decided to put on every Christmas.

I decided to write a Nativity Play myself, and this was when, although I did not realise it at the time, I began to learn the pitfalls of written drama. My play was never finished and never performed. At the age of ten, I was possibly too young to attempt a play, as my mental capability to carry an idea was still developing. Here is an example of what I wrote:

Scene Two. THE SHEPHERDS.

ANGEL: Go to Bethlehem. A Child has been born.
He is your Saviour.

SHEPHERDS: We will.
  (They go)

Now, we can learn several things from this. First that I was
unable to think of anything for the characters to say. I had
been unable to grasp, at the age of ten, that my Shepherds
and my Angel were *real*.

Any person, king or peasant, butler or murderer, who
appears in your play must be a character with a life of his
or her own, not a cardboard cut-out. Once you have grasped
that it is *real people* you are writing about, that they were
busy doing something half an hour before they made their
entrance onto the stage, that they too slept last night, possibly had toothache last week and dreaded their visit to the
dentist – in short – are human beings rather than things to
be manipulated, you should find they will begin to come up
with their own lines as their characters dictate.

The second thing we can learn from my Nativity Play is
the importance of setting the *scene* (which I had neglected
to do). How you go about setting the scene can vary: Shaw
wrote quite lengthy descriptions of his sets; David Campton,
who is currently writing some of the best plays for the
amateur theatre, often hardly sketches in the background.
But you must have a clear picture in your mind of *where*
your play is taking place. Even if it is in some remote region
like Heaven or Hell, the setting must be real to you. No
use writing hopefully: 'The scene is Heaven.' Producers will
want to know concrete details to transfer to their stages.
What does Heaven look like? Are there any chairs? Is it
indoors or out-of-doors?

The third point we can learn from my example concerns
a vital ingredient in every piece of successful drama. It is
conflict, and a good rule to remember is: 'Drama *is* conflict.'
It's what every play must be about.

14

Anyone of any intelligence knows that conflict means contrast, argument, fighting, confrontations, disturbances. But you may be a little bewildered, because some plays don't seem to contain any of these things. Take Samuel Beckett's *Waiting for Godot*. This, on the surface, is a long play where nothing seems to happen. The characters are waiting for a person who never comes. And then what about, for instance, a hilarious comedy? There may appear to be no conflict in, say, a Whitehall farce.

But conflict does not just mean physical fighting or argument. It is the way in which the characters react to each other. My brief scene from my Nativity Play is absolutely lifeless. But what if I had written it like this?

Scene Two. THE SHEPHERDS.

ANGEL: Go to Bethlehem. A Child has been born. He is your Saviour.

FIRST SHEPHERD: How can we believe that? And who are you, anyway?

SECOND SHEPHERD: Don't you see, he's an angel. We must have faith. Let's go.
  (They go)

Here, an element of conflict has been introduced. One of the characters doubts the word of the Angel. Straight away, this tiny fragment leaps to life. We know immediately that the Second Shepherd has a greater belief in miracles. Even in two lines, they have become real, and interest has been created.

The conflict may be much more subtle than this, but don't worry about trying to introduce complicated undertones into your play at this stage. Don't force anything. I mention only to show you the range of possibilities open, that there can be physical conflict, verbal conflict, mental or emotional

15

conflict. In *Waiting for Godot* the conflict is between the characters and the seeming futility of their situation.

To sum up the rules so far, then, your play must be about *real people,* it must be set in a specific *place* you can describe (if you need to) and the action must contain some sort of *conflict.*

Time

Sometimes in books on playwriting, you will come across references to mysterious things called Unities. The Unity of Time, the Unity of Place, the Unity of Action. These are elaborations of the work of Aristotle, particularly his views on tragedy, and need not have anything to do with your play as such, though some comments on Time, Place and Personality do require mentioning here.

So far as Time is concerned, unless you are writing a fantasy or some sort of cavalcade of events, you should at least at this early stage in your career, keep the time covered in real life by the performance of a one-act half-hour play, to about the same amount of time in the story you are telling. Do not, for instance, attempt to show the happenings of ten minutes, then skip two months to detail something that happened two months later, and then leap a gap of twenty years in order to let the last ten minutes of the play take place when the characters are middle-aged.

Remember that it is difficult to fake time convincingly on a stage. You can, of course, have a change of scene or a blackout to indicate the passing of time, but this is not advisable in a one-act play. The structure will not stand it. Later we will examine how a one-act play is constructed, but for the time being, try to keep your ideas for the action of a one-act play to the realms of half-an-hour's happenings in the lives of your characters. You can stretch this to perhaps an hour – stage meals, for instance, are much smaller and are over much quicker than meals in real life; and the audience will accept that a character has run to the Post Office, queued for a postal order and then run back, even if he has only been off the stage for five minutes. But this means that during the length of your play, the characters must live out your whole plot, and probably a good deal will happen that would take much longer if it were actually true.

Even if your play is to be full-length with a running time of two hours or so, which is the average for a Two or Three-Act script, keep the action to the 'nitty gritty' of the drama that is working itself out rather than filling up your First Act with a lot of introduction about the events that have led up to the situation which you intend should grip the audience. It is not advisable to have each of your Acts set 'Ten years later'. A play should be concentrated, a few highly-charged hours (or days) in the lives of your characters rather than a long-drawn-out affair which plods on for thirty years.

Look at the way Shakespeare tackled the question of Time in *Romeo and Juliet*. Nowadays a playwright would not use a Prologue, but even if the Bard had dispensed with his opening explanation about the feud between the houses of Montague and Capulet, it wouldn't have mattered, as he skilfully made sure, when two of the Capulet servants entered in his opening scene, that they let us know what would happen if they chanced to bump into any of those 'dogs' of Montagues. A lesser playwright might have decided the feud needed a lot of introduction, and used up half the First Act showing the audience just how it had come about, but Shakespeare concentrated his play on the dramatic short period when the young heir and heiress to the feuding houses lived out their brief and tragic passion that was to break the feud at the expense of their lives.

In *The Taming of the Shrew*, he lets Lucentio explain in the first speech of the play proper just what he is doing in Padua, where he has come from, and what his father thought about it. Such directness is not suitable for a modern play,

17

but you can bear in mind that often the characters may not know each other when they make their entrances, so it is perfectly reasonable for them to ask each other questions. Or you may set the play in, say, the foyer of a hotel, where everyone who comes in has to register at the desk. In this way, the audience will learn by the way they announce themselves and what they say to their companions or the hotel staff, who they are and why they are present and what might have happened previously.

Place

The place where your play is set is subject to the same restrictions as the time. Obviously if the play takes place in one room, the audience cannot see anything that happens off-stage in some other part of the 'house', and there is no way you can overcome this unless you have a multiple set which shows a section of the whole house or a gauze (which can be lit from behind and can then be seen through, or if lit from in front, will appear solid) letting us see an inner chamber.

Therefore the whole of the play must take place in this particular setting, or if you are writing a full-length script, in no more than two or three settings – and even if you have two or three, you cannot use them all together, you are limited to the set on the stage at that particular moment in the play.

So whether your set is a room, a rocky hillside or a prison cell, you have to find reasonable excuses for anyone who is present on the stage to be there, and sometimes your characters will have to say things they would normally have said in some other place to each other, so you must make this believable.

As with time, when the characters can refer to what happened last week or last year, you can also describe events off-stage in the dialogue. In a play about the French Revolution, for instance, you might open with a woman waiting in a room. When the second character enters, the woman runs to her:

> Where have you been? I was so worried. And what in heaven's name has happened to you? There's blood on your face, and you've lost your bonnet.

The second person might then reply:

> Oh, Marie, terrible things are going on. They say the people are storming the Bastille. I had to struggle through the crowds, and somebody caught me with a stone – they're all like mad creatures, the men are beasts, but the women are even worse. We must leave Paris.

This little interchange has opened up the action so that we see not only the room, we are aware that outside is the terror-filled Paris of the Revolution. Off-stage sound effects can assist this illusion, but do not rely on them too much. In this case, for instance, a few bursts of shouting can make one of the characters say desperately, as she looks out of a 'window':

> I hope the crowds aren't coming this way – No, they're going past the the end of the street.

Always, however, you must remember that what is important is what is happening on the stage before our eyes, and nothing of vital relevance to the plot should take place 'off'. As an example of this I want to tell you about a production I once saw of an adaptation of *Wuthering Heights*. This was a lamentable failure, and it was all the author's fault since he hadn't tried to think of any way of taking us out on the moors or down to Thrushcross Grange. The whole of the long First Act was set in the kitchen of the Heights itself, and so the famous scene where Cathy and Heathcliff look through the windows of the Grange and are attacked by dogs, with the result that Cathy is wounded and has to be left at the Grange to recover, took place 'off'. We never saw any of it, the author had given Heathcliff a long speech when he came back to the Heights, where he simply told the story of what had happened.

Nothing is so vivid or convincing at second-hand as it is when we see it with our own eyes. In this case, we should have been *shown* that vital scene of contrast between the gypsyish figures from the Heights and the elegant people at the Grange. Never, never let any important piece of the action take place 'off', unless it is something like the birth of a child or a gruesome operation, which cannot reasonably be expected to be shown in gory detail. In a play, you should always *show* important events or points, not just let the characters tell them.

Personality

As the characters in your play are real people, you must bear in mind that they will develop in the way that real people do, especially under stress. If your play is about some deeply traumatic event such as the French Revolution, the audience may find that a person who at first appeared shy and insignificant, for instance, will turn out to have far greater resources of courage than one who seemed more confident and sure of herself. This happens all the time in real life, and though of course a play is not real, it is based on reality, so the more human you can make your characters, the greater depth and impact your play will have.

It will help you if you try to cultivate the habit of being aware of people around you, what they are doing and saying. Listen in to conversations unashamedly, on buses, in trains, in crowded supermarkets. Try to work out why so-and-so took such a seemingly uncharacteristic action instead of behaving as you would have expected. Remember that your characters, too, as well as real people, might be suffering from indigestion, toothache, a bad back, or marital problems. Naturally, they will have to reveal this to the other characters and the audience in the course of events, or else their odd behaviour will remain a mystery (though in real life, of course, people often do not explain such things, which is why art is far more satisfying; some reason is always given sooner or later to make mysteries solve themselves.)

Each of your characters must be believable and convincing, even the unpleasant ones. After all, even the nastiest person understands himself to a certain degree; even a murderer believes he has some reason for his actions; every human being feels justified in taking whatever course of action he might take over anything.

The autocratic head of a business, whom you present in your play as a forceful and domineering personality, may be deeply worried in private about his bank balance or his marriage, or may suffer agonies of insecurity, and you should try to bear the whole person in mind when writing your play, not just one aspect of him.

One point to note, though, is that in plays, little portraits of 'types' are often used. If you have watched stage plays, you may recognise some of them – the 'typical' char, the postman, the doctor, the bossy Lady of the Manor. These are what actors would describe as 'stock' or 'cameo parts'. They are characters who generally appear quite briefly, and so do not develop into deep or complex individuals. They always stay the same, they never do anything unexpected, they behave exactly the way we would expect them to and never surprise us.

Using 'stock' characters is a useful method of giving an audience a rest for a few moments, as they will understand without having to be told that they can simply accept such people at their face value, and do not have to watch or listen carefully for hidden depths. Even in a very serious play, 'stock' characters can help to provide variety, and can be used to relieve tension after, perhaps, a confrontation between deeper and more complex characters.

Usually, 'stock' people are inclined to be on the humorous side because they are completely unaware of any undercurrents or emotions in whoever they are talking to and they take it for granted that everyone is as uncomplicated as they are themselves.

The Porter in Act II of *Macbeth* is a 'stock' character, a garrulous, drunken old man who wants to ramble on about his own particular philosophies on drink even while, around him, murder is being done and terrible events are occurring. So wrapped up in himself and his own affairs, he provides a welcome break for a few moments for the audience after the tense scene of Duncan's murder and before events in the form of MacDuff begin to stalk the guilty Macbeth and his wife.

A word of warning though. A play filled with 'stock' characters will be wooden and unreal – unless you are writing a farce, where it is necessary for the characters to be rather shallow – and you will generally require at least some of your characters to have a certain amount of depth.

Chapter Three

THE CONSTRUCTION OF A PLAY

The blueprint you construct for the guidance of the players who will interpret your play has, in the same way as a bridgebuilder's plan of his bridge, got to have a definite shape to it. His bridge is probably going to be in the form of an arch, solidly fixed to terra firma at each end, but soaring gracefully from one side to the other. Your play has a different shape. The easiest way to think of it is as a kind of graph, a type of temperature chart which rises in a series of leaps to its highest point at the end. The leaps do not indicate a nasty increase in feverishness, but an increase in the power of your play to grip and hold the audience.

When the curtain rises in a theatre, the audience, who might well have paid fairly substantially for their seats in the auditorium, are in a mood of pleasant expectancy. They have come to the theatre to be entertained, and they are willing and ready to be pleased by what they see and interested in it. Within the first few moments, they will wriggle a bit and sigh as they make themselves comfortable, but if the play has been properly constructed, they should be swept up almost from the opening lines so that they quickly become absorbed, so much so that the reality of the theatre around them is forgotten, the make-believe world you have created for them on the stage is all-important. If you can hold them in this suspension of disbelief, turning the screw, as it were, a little tighter as the play progresses, bit by bit, they will have to blink several times after the final curtain has fallen in order to bring themselves back from the vividness of what has happened on the stage to your characters, to the realisation that they have got to go out and find their cars, catch their buses or whatever, and wake from the dream. The experience will have been successful and rewarding for everyone concerned, and, as the initiator of the whole thing, you can feel rather smug because you have written such a skilful blueprint which masterminded it all. In other words, such a good play.

How do you achieve this miracle?

Well, in the first place, your play needs to have some sort of story to it, however slight. The story is generally referred to as the plot, but there are plays which do not seem to have a definite story to them – plays of mood or thought. These are very difficult to handle, so you will be wise to make sure that your first attempts at playwriting are not about shifting relationships or changing points of view, but about a series of events or happenings, ideally with a neat and satisfactory 'twist' at the end.

The action in which the audience will be so interested should begin to get under way from the very first page, whether the play is funny, serious or sad, and it needs to build up (like the leaps on the temperature chart) to a climax at the end. In between the beginning and the end come other, lesser climaxes, with moments of calm interspersed.

Some people imagine that a one-act play and a full-length play are the same thing, except that the one-act play is shorter (and therefore, they think, easier to write) but each of them has its own special 'temperature chart' that makes the construction rather different.

The One-Act Play

Ideally, a one-act play should be compact, a single unit with no time lapses, pauses for the scenery to be changed or

24

intervals to distract the audience from becoming fully involved, once the play has begun and they have settled down, until the play is over and the curtain falls at the end. During this time – half-an-hour or so – the playwright must first of all gain their interest and attention for the situation he introduces to them and the story he is about to tell, and then proceed through two or three major climaxes to the final climax at the end, which will resolve the whole thing and leave the audience satisfied at the outcome. There may be room in a one-act play for quite a few smaller climaxes in between the large ones as well as moments of rest for the characters and the audience, but by and large, the 'temperature chart' of a one-act play should look like the graph in

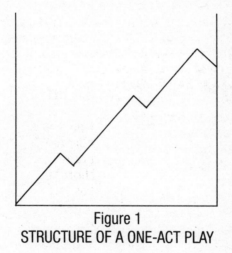

Figure 1
STRUCTURE OF A ONE-ACT PLAY

Naturally the events of the plot, and how this affects the characters, will help to grip the audience, but we are concerned here with the actual construction, the way in which the bits of the play are put together in the right order so that the graph continues to rise and the interest is held all the way through. The best way I can illustrate this is to

25

examine a one-act play to see how the playwright has worked at crafting climaxes in an effective manner.

A Fishy Business by Margaret Wood (published by Samuel French) is an excellent example of a well-constructed play. There is one setting, the sitting room of a house, and the whole action takes place just before and during a dinner-party given by the occupants of the house, a likeable though rather harassed couple, George and Mary. So here, the limitations of place and time have been met satisfactorily, and there will be no scene changes, lapses of hours (or days!) or any other delays to stop the audience from being swept along with increasing interest once the play has begun.

This is a comedy – though not a farce – and so the characters display naturalistic and human qualities: they get bothered, irritated, they worry about the disasters which (from the first few lines) threaten to beset the evening. Small problems are mentioned first as Mary tries to hurry her husband into getting ready for the occasion. George is grumpy as Mary talks in wheedling 'baby-talk' (off-stage) to the cat, then the tension of preparing for the evening – which the audience will recognise with amusement – gets to both of them, and when George does go off to get dressed, he finds his shirt has both buttons missing from the cuffs. At this point, the first climax of the play occurs.

Mary has set the table 'off', and comes rushing screaming for her husband, carrying the dish. Disaster! The fresh salmon caught by Uncle Richard, who is to be one of the guests at the dinner-party, has been ruined. The middle of it has been eaten – somehow the cat has got at it. What can be done – apart from George threatening the cat with muttered curses and throwing it out in disgrace?

Calm is restored somewhat (and the 'graph' falls a little from the first 'peak' on the temperature chart) as the distraught host and hostess decide to fill in the gap with tinned salmon, cover it up with greenstuff, and make sure they serve that portion to themselves. Smaller conflicts and climaxes are hinted at during the conversation, since another of the guests is a domestic science teacher, and Mary feels her last-ditch effort with the greenstuff will disgrace her in Miss Wagstaffe's eyes if the teacher ever finds out about the bungled meal. And what if Uncle Richard should suspect? Still, they think, reassuring each other, he'll be too busy telling the other guests how he caught the darned thing to notice. Prepared for the fray, they scurry on with their last-minute preparations just as the guests begin to arrive.

The entry of the guests creates interest, but you should note that a new character appearing in the course of a play does not mark a climax unless they have some spectacular news to tell, or are assumed to be dead, or something of that sort. In this case, their entries – first the Vicar and his wife, then Miss Wagstaffe, lastly Uncle Richard – keep the action moving and the conversation flowing and provide a little series of minor 'ups and downs' such as when the Vicar, left alone with his wife for a few speeches, expresses regret at the fact that they are apparently going to be served a cold supper rather than the roast they had expected, and he and his wife privately deplore the meanness of their hosts over what they consider to be inferior sherry served to them.

During this part of the play, the playwright is dropping hints, which will keep the tension already created in the minds of the audience – the Vicar's wife asks after the cat; Miss Wagstaffe declares she is anticipating a delicious meal and that being a domestic science teacher isn't everything; Uncle Richard and Miss Wagstaffe, flirting coyly with each other, end by acting out the way in which a fish should be successfully caught. The playwright also makes sure that further developments in the action are anticipated – the Vicar's wife enquires after George and Mary's son Nigel, and we discover that he is something of a 'drop-out' at University. This is important since Nigel and his girl-friend will enter later, when the dinner is under way in the dining-room 'off', so the ground has been prepared.

Things are building up very quietly to the next big climax,

and the audience will be waiting expectantly to see what this will be. Will the guests discover the deception over the salmon? What will happen? Obviously something is going to go wrong, and the longer things seem to be going reasonably well, the greater becomes the anticipation of the enthralled audience.

When the guests disappear 'off' to sit down for their meal, enter Nigel and his girlfriend Felicity to occupy the now empty stage. The contrast between their amusing inanities and the social chit-chat of the guests previously gives yet another dimension to the comedy of the play, and as George and Mary pass through the room with empty plates, worrying about the sweet and the coffee, the action keeps moving as they exchange talk between Nigel and themselves. In the end, after trying unsuccessfully to borrow some money from his father for fish and chips (since food has not been provided for him in all the worry over the dinner for the guests) and upsetting the diners in the other room by playing noisy pop music, Nigel is given the remains of the salmon from the party to finish up, he and Felicity eat it between them, and they decide to leave for a 'demo'.

Still the tension is mounting, the graph is rising. Nothing has gone wrong so far, even Nigel hasn't succeeded in spoiling the evening. Will George and Mary make it successfully to where they can see their guests out? The suspense (the audience feels) is becoming unbearable.

Then, as Mary is collecting the milk from the doorstep to make the coffee, and the guests are wading (off-stage) into the sweet, the crunch comes. Mary calls George from the dining-room to tell him in a hysterical whisper that she has found the cat dead on the doorstep. The graph rises sharply as they discuss what has happened in increasingly alarmed horror. The cat must have been poisoned! It was the salmon! And all their guests have eaten it!

Unaware, the satisfied guests emerge for coffee in the sitting room as George and Mary try to pretend that everything is normal, but compliments about the unusual taste of

28

the fish arouse in George and Mary a guilty need to find out whether everyone feels quite well. Once they have established that their guests are fine, and have in the process succeeded in arousing a suspicious wonder as to why all these odd questions are being asked, they reveal what has happened, but say comfortingly that if everyone is okay, no harm has been done.

The graph is now rising high as the climax mounts. In turn, the guests begin to turn green at the thought that they have eaten salmon which poisoned the cat, they accuse each other of making matters worse, they stagger out in turns to the bathroom while the ambulance is summoned. Smaller climaxes are added to the major one. Uncle Richard reveals that he didn't catch the salmon at all, he bought it to give credibility to all his 'fishy' stories which nobody would believe. Ambulance-men appear on the scene and the weakly indignant guests are taken away on stretchers, leaving Mary and George to sink down to recover. The graph begins to fall, but all is not yet over. Mary suddenly remembers that Nigel and Felicity have eaten the salmon as well. She is bemoaning the fact that her son is probably lying in agony somewhere when the door slams, and in walks Nigel himself.

Quickly the last climax which gives the 'twist' to the play comes as Mary and George question him frantically. What a night, he declares, first the cat and then – Yes, when Nigel and Felicity went off to the 'demo', he took the family car (which was mentioned with some indignation by George at the time) and accidentally killed the cat which was, though he didn't know, underneath it. Unwilling to spoil the evening with the little tragedy, he left Tiddles on the doorstep with a note beneath the corpse explaining – a note which Mary, in her agitation, never found. As the graph begins to fall from this last peak of action, George declares that it serves all the guests right, since they weren't true friends anyway, they hadn't been poisoned at all and nothing had been wrong with the evening's hospitality. The tension is broken, and on a scene of Mary's collapse into wailing, George and his son (united for once) share a welcome drink and the curtain falls.

You will see that the incidents in a one-act play and the whole of the action must be carefully linked together so that everything leads up to the final climax, whether this is what the audience are expecting or not. Nothing must be included which does not have some relevance to the main theme; the audience must not be distracted by interesting sidelines which are afterwards left hanging in the air, as it were. And you hold the attention of your audience by playing on their anticipation, their expectancy, their curiosity.

If you examine any good one-act play, you will see that it has been crafted so that at the very beginning, some sort of question is posed. Even if the play is one of relationships rather than action, the playwright must always indicate as soon as possible that something is about to happen – there is a problem to be solved, an obstacle to be overcome, an answer to be discovered, a threat to be evaded. And it is by means of the way in which your characters cope with what we will for the sake of convenience refer to as the Question (whether this is actually a problem, an obstacle, a threat or whatever) that you keep the audience's attention. They will want to know whether the Question is going to be satisfactorily resolved, and if, in the course of the action, you give only part of the answer away – then, later, another little bit – their expectation, never quite satisfied, will mount with each frustration of their desire to feel everything has been sorted out, to fever pitch. Each climax should embroil them further in the complications of the Question – or some new aspect of the Question coming to light – or what seemed as though it might be the answer only leads to further confusion – until by the time the climax at the end is approaching, they are sitting on the edges of their seats, biting their nails, hardly able to stand the suspense.

At the end, the playwright puts them out of their misery. The climax comes, the Question is answered in full, there are no loose ends, everything is tied up, it's all over. They sink back, feeling they have been through a most gripping experience. Even if the play is a comedy, they should experience the same sense of relief as if the Question concerned some awful crime or a terrible revelation that the boss's secretary (who seemed so normal) was actually going mad, or the wife's discovery that she could no longer stand her husband, and her decision to leave him. Whatever the play is about, you hold the attention of the audience by the same method – let them see the Question or guess at it – and then keep them wondering, worrying, hoping, praying, dying to know – their involvement and curiosity mounting by means of your graph to that final climax which will reveal all, and leave them free to recover (and to tell each other how much they enjoyed the play and what a wonderful playwright you are!)

The Full-length Play

Since a full-length play runs for two hours or longer, and is split up into Acts (possibly Scenes as well) with at least one interval, and maybe a few five-minute breaks while the set is being re-dressed for the next Scene, its graph rises in a slightly different manner.

Any interval or fall of the curtain breaks the concentration of the audience, and gives them the opportunity to withdraw, for however short a time, from the clutches of the world you have created for them. They will consult the programme, wriggle their toes because their shoes are too tight, remember the gas bill that came in the morning post, or talk to their companion. When the curtain rises again, it will take them some minutes to settle down and be drawn into the activities of your characters once more.

The first Act should therefore build up to a climax in the same sort of way a one-act play does, but ideally, the climax should be one which only seems to open up further complications – so that the audience cannot wait to see what will happen in the next Act. If there are three Acts, the second one picks up afresh and builds up with another rising graph to an even more frustrating climax, so this time the audience is all agog for the revelations and answers that will – they confidently expect – astound and delight them when all is revealed as the final Act builds up to the great denouement, surprise, or whatever is to crown the whole play at the end.

The graph of a full-length (two- or three-Act) play should therefore look something like the examples in Figure 2 (overleaf).

Even in a full-length play, the playwright has to pose a Question (problem, obstacle, threat or whatever) right at the beginning, so that the audience will become intrigued. Obviously, however, the Question can be a more compli-cated one than can be satisfactorily resolved within the con-fines of a one-act play, and generally, in a full-length work, there are at least one or two secondary Questions (often called sub-plots) that are entwined with the primary one and can help or hinder the satisfactory resolution of the main theme as the play progresses. The sub-plots usually involve supporting characters, not the main protagonists.

To illustrate this, let us look at a full-length play and examine its construction. The one I have chosen is J. B. Priestley's celebrated 'Yorkshire Farcical Comedy' *When We Are Married* (published by Samuel French).

This is written in three Acts, but the playwright has skil-fully worked out the structure so that there is only one set throughout (no difficult scene changes) and the intervals of time between the Acts are a mere half-hour between Acts One and Two, and quarter of an hour between Acts Two and Three. The whole play therefore keeps as unified as possible with regard to place and time – the action covers the traumatic events of one evening, no 'years later', or ten different sets for a lot of small scenes.

The main Question which arises to confound the principal characters – three local worthies and their wives who are

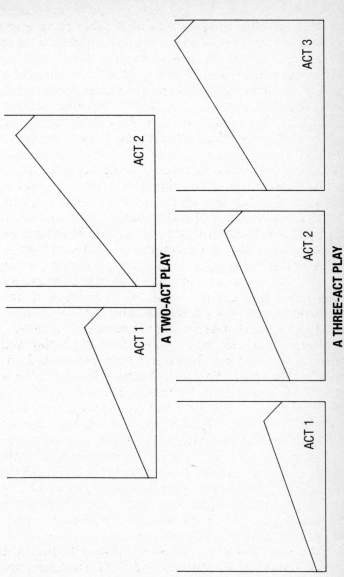

A TWO-ACT PLAY

A THREE-ACT PLAY

Figure 2 STRUCTURES OF FULL-LENGTH PLAYS

celebrating their Silver Wedding, having all got married together on the same morning twenty-five years previously – is the staggering revelation that the young clergyman who conducted the ceremony discovered afterwards that he hadn't filled in all the right documents to make him qualified to unite them in matrimony. This, it seems, had only affected two marriages, but the triple wedding had been one of them. The Question, then, is, what can be done, since all three gentlemen (and their wives) are pillars of respectability, and it now appears they have been living in sin for twenty-five years – a thought that is too appalling to contemplate.

Worked in with the way the main Question is revealed – the means by which the truth is made known, in fact – is a secondary Question involving the young organist of the church. He and the niece of Alderman Helliwell, one of the 'worthies', are in love and 'walking out' together. They have been seen, and Gerald, the young man, is now considered unsuitable for the post of organist, so the 'worthies', in their dignified respectability, want to dismiss him. So the secondary Question is, will Gerald actually be dismissed, and will he and his sweetheart Nancy have to part?

Other sub-plots are skilfully introduced when two gentlemen of the press arrive to 'write up' and photograph the six who are celebrating their Silver Wedding – in the end, it is revealed that one of these gentlemen was the bridegroom in the second 'fake' marriage ceremony performed by the unfortunate young clergyman, and that though he has been trying for years to free himself from his wife, his marriage certificate is only too legal because it was also signed by the registrar as well as the clergyman. Which means – as they all realise with great sighs of relief – that everyone had been legally married all the time.

Interest is built up in each Act and the first curtain falls after the three gentlemen are informed they have unknowingly been living in sin. They depart to consider what to do about it – little realising that the 'help', Mrs Northrop, has

34

been listening at the door and has heard everything. And Mrs Northrop, who is also under threat of dismissal because she isn't 'satisfactory', will make sure, the audience realises with fascinated horror, that the awful truth will be spread far and wide.

In Act Two, Mrs Northrop attempts a little blackmail to keep the secret, and things seem to go from bad to worse. Bumbling attempts are made to try and sort out the situation, and the second climax comes as even more skeletons tumble out of the family cupboards. A 'lady friend' of Alderman Helliwell arrives to enquire into the new state of affairs, since, she claims, he's often told her that if only he was free, he would marry her, so now that he apparently is . . . ?

By Act Three, the wives are beginning to wonder whether they even want to stay married (or be re-married) and they tell their husbands some home truths which they have never dared to reveal before about their men being boring, stingy – and generally, with their unaccustomed freedom going to their heads, they start to stand up for their rights to a little consideration. When it is finally discovered that the marriages were all legal after all, the situation is very different from the self-satisfied, respectable and pompous group presented at the beginning of the play, and the audience has the satisfactory feeling that the upset has probably done them all a lot of good.

The secondary Questions are all neatly tied up too, of course, and the play ends.

Naturally, not every play ever written will fit exactly into the forms of construction I have outlined here. Shakespeare used five Acts, not three, and even today, there are exceptions to the rule – hour-long plays which are neither one-act nor full-length, strictly speaking, or entertainments which do not consist of acts, but of linked short scenes, possibly on a common theme. Generally, however, anything that you might come across which seems to prove to you that there is no need to follow any rules and you can do exactly as

35

you like, will be the work of playwrights who mastered technique first before they decided to invent their own forms of drama.

There is nothing to stop you from doing your own thing either, but without craftsmanship and skill and an understanding of what you are doing and why, your play (or whatever it is) will almost certainly never make that vital leap from the page, far less be able to sweep your audience along with it as it unfolds on the stage itself.

Chapter Four

THE PLOT

It will now be obvious that the story of your play – the plot – needs to be carefully worked out so that it will have the best possible effect on the audience, and engage their attention, holding this through the sorts of climaxes I have mentioned, until the final curtain has fallen. A sequence of events, however amusing or amazing, such as might occur in real life, cannot be used 'just as they happened' to you or to people you know, since real life has no plot, there are always loose ends and threads which remain unresolved. Any incident or happening can, however, be used as the basis for your plot, or incorporated into it, so long as you can see clearly the pattern of the play as a whole, and the essential artificiality which is involved in the construction of a play. Hardly anything in real life has a distinct beginning, middle and end, and your play must possess all three.

Originality

Nobody can tell you how to think of your own plot, whether of a one-act or full-length play or anything else. It has to be your own creation, the product of your very original and special brain and your own particular way of looking at the world and the people in it. The most that anybody else can do is to give you a thought, a basic idea, an interesting point, which will kindle your inventiveness and enthusiasm so that you just can't wait to get to work.

You may worry, however, because your plot – your own hard-thought-out, much worked-over story for your play – seems rather similar to other plays you have seen or heard of, or is contemptuously dismissed by the people you hesitantly show it to as 'unoriginal'. So let's get one fact clear here and now. There is no new situation, no completely fresh and unheard-of story which you have somehow got to try and discover. Every idea that could possibly be thought of has already been used somewhere by somebody.

Originality does not lie in inventing a plot that has absolutely no connection at all with anything else that has ever been written. Your play will, I can assure you, be 'original' purely because you, rather than Sheridan or Pinter or Robert Bolt or anyone else you can think of, are the author. Whether you are aware of it or not, you are a unique person; there is not, never has been and never will be, anybody who thinks, feels and writes in the way you do, which is entirely and absolutely original to you. So have confidence in yourself and take no notice of anyone who shakes their head over your idea and mutters darkly that it's 'the old eternal triangle again' or 'just another version of Romeo and Juliet'. They are only revealing their ignorance of what all art is about.

The 'eternal triangle', 'Romeo and Juliet', the 'Cinderella story', 'local boy makes good', 'love overcomes all', 'good overcomes evil' – all these are just shorthand formulae we use to denote the great themes, the eternal struggles, which have beset humanity ever since our ancestors first crawled out of their swamp and started to try and cope with the fact that they were human beings, with fears, hopes, ideals and dreams.

If your play is based on the 'Cinderella story' – and why not, there's no reason at all why you shouldn't transfer it, in your own way, to the setting of a mill town and the Mill Owner falling for the little girl at her loom, or the Wild

West with the wealthy rancher and the saloon floozy – it will still be 'original' because you have worked your own plot out and presented your own ideas and thoughts on this particular situation.

When you are working out your plot – or even trying to think of one – remember that there is no copyright on situations, or even on other people's themes, so long as you don't actually copy another play word for word, or use the exact techniques and developments some other author used, then claim you thought them up yourself.

But take the story of Romeo and Juliet, basically that of young lovers divided by conflicting loyalties. It wasn't 'original' to Shakespeare, he picked up the theme from somewhere else, and after him there have been countless other playwrights who have felt they wanted to say something on the subject of young love trapped by divided loyalty. Yvonne Mitchell set the story between a Jewish and a Christian family in London in *The Same Sky*; *West Side Story* transferred it to New York. No doubt someone will eventually place it – if they haven't done so already – on a space station between a young heroine from Earth and a hero from Mars who feel that space and planetary differences are no barrier to true love.

Such recurring themes never die because inherent in them all is what we have already seen to be the basis of drama – conflict. And whether the conflict is between young lovers fighting tradition and authority for their right to be happy, or a struggle between the 'right' and the 'wrong' woman to win the man they both want, it doesn't matter how many times the audience has seen this situation before, they will still be avidly interested in what you, in your own special way, have to say about it.

If you feel you cannot think of a plot for your play, and your mind stubbornly remains a blank, you might well find, as some of the greatest modern playwrights have done, that other people's plays will spark off an idea. Peter Ustinov

39

turned the tragedy of Romeo and Juliet into uproar in his comedy *Romanoff And Juliet*; Tom Stoppard examined the private lives of the characters who appear in *Hamlet* in his *Rosencrantz And Guildenstern Are Dead*; Eugene O'Neill went back to Greek drama for the theme of *Mourning Becomes Electra* – and on a less weighty note, I once appeared in a play, the title of which I have forgotten, where Cinderella and Prince Charming, twenty years after their romance in the fairy-tale, were comfortably middle-aged and trying to cope with their headstrong young daughter who was determined – much to the royal horror – to marry a plumber! In the end, when there was a flood from burst pipes in the Palace, the plumber saved the situation and so won the hand of the Princess!

Other people's work, snippets in a newspaper, historical incidents – the idea for your play may come from anywhere at all, even, possibly, something so prosaic as a Plumber's Manual!

Conflict

So you have your idea, you are ready to begin detailed work on the story you've got in mind for your play – the plot. You know the scene, the time, the people. Now for the what and the why and the how – the ways in which the Question is going to be posed at the beginning of your play to arrest your audience, and the devious methods by which it will eventually be resolved to everyone's satisfaction.

I have already mentioned that the most important element in any play is *conflict*. Indeed, the introduction of what we have called the Question (problem, obstacle, threat or whatever) – including secondary Questions in a full-length play – presupposes quite a good deal of conflict, since the solving of a problem, the overcoming of an obstacle, the evasion of a threat, will all involve your characters in confrontations, questions, discoveries and other disrupting

40

activities. You will also have become aware by now why it is to your benefit – in your early attempts at writing a play anyway – to avoid plays of idea and mood and to keep to a fairly strong storyline with lots of little incidents to carry the play forward. I suggest too that you make your cast reasonably large, not keep it to two or three characters, because if they have to carry the whole burden of the play, you might well find yourself scratching your head and wondering what on earth they can say to each other next. Sustained dialogue is not easy to invent – good sustained dialogue, that is – and it will be fatal if you resort to trivial chit-chat that has no bearing on the plot in order to fill up the pages of your blueprint. Every word in a play must count, everything you include in it must be there for a purpose, otherwise the audience will lose interest and begin to yawn and your graph, far from building up to the stunning climax, will belly-flop disastrously.

Do not imagine, though, that your play will be filled with conflict if your characters merely yell abuse at each other throughout, or take sides and argue. That sort of thing has its place, but it's far more likely to be in, say, a debate, or even on the football terraces. Though differences of opinion can be exciting and argument can be stimulating, they will produce only boredom in the onlooker if they just go on and on with no let-up or variation. So if you were beginning to think along those lines, a word of warning. . .

I'd like to point out here a mistake sometimes made by people who are perhaps too cerebral in their approach. Their plays are very civilized, and there are no raised voices, but often the characters are simply mouthpieces for some sort of message or conviction that the author wants to explain to the audience. Earnest discussion, even if the characters do not agree with each other and however erudite and witty the dialogue, does not make for a good play either. Many great plays do contain messages or comments which make the audience stop and think, but first and foremost, they are successful examples of this particular art form

41

– the artificially constructed framework of a stage play that will grab its audience and keep them enthralled until the final curtain. So do not use the medium of your play to try and put across your own personal convictions – if they are introduced into the plot later, when the basic structure is settled and clear, all well and good, but get the shape of your play and your graph worked out first; do all the carpentry, as it were, before you try to stun your audience with your opinions on the state of the world or the problems of humanity.

You will find it much easier if, by and large, you are more concerned as you write with what happened next rather than what people said next. But remember that each A4 page, though it might take you half an hour to write, will take only two minutes to be acted out, so don't have 'happenings' every few lines so that your characters are dashing up and down and on and off the stage like the characters in a jerky, flickery old film.

Even in a play filled with conflict and action, these elements don't necessarily have to be physical, your characters don't have to leap in through windows in order to surprise the villains, attack each other, or throw things. Neither does the conflict have to come from without in the form of revolution, escaped convicts, raiders with guns or ransacking mobs. Several pages, for example, might be spent with your characters sitting in armchairs considering the Question (whatever this is) and what on earth they can do about it. Suggestions might be put forward, discussed, reluctantly discarded. Further action could take place if they are forced to try and keep the Question from being discovered by other characters – the conversation as they try to divert the newcomers away from dangerous ground – attempts to try and persuade Mother and Aunt Maud that the ladies are tired after their journey and need a rest before anything at all is discussed ('anything at all' here meaning, obviously, the Question). Mother and Aunt, equally determinedly, insist they want to know here and now, just exactly What is Going On.

I have already mentioned that there are other sorts of conflict apart from fighting and confrontations; verbal, emotional, mental. And though your characters have to act out your plot, they must always seem real to the audience. Certain methodical people may possibly feel that by working their story out in minute detail, with everything neatly labelled, tabulated and explained, every entrance and exit planned as though by computer, the whole dovetailed with microscopic precision, their play needs very little else adding to it – it must, they feel, be good since it rests on such a strong framework.

But quite often in these cases, if you read or watch such a play, you will become aware of a certain disquiet because the characters seem to say only the absolute minimum necessary to clarify the exposition of the plot, and they don't seem like people at all, but like puppets being moved by a puppeteer or figures on a chess-board. What the author has overlooked is that as well as including conflict in the plot, or posing his Question and taking us through the story until everything is resolved, he should have recollected that a great deal of conflict can come from the interaction of the characters and the ways in which they respond as individuals. The plot is the skeleton of a play, but no audience wants to sit and look at a set of bare bones. Your characters are the flesh and blood, they will quarrel, disagree, love, hate, generally fill out the framework of the plot and make the audience believe the happenings of your play are utterly convincing.

So even though you might have in your mind the question: *what will happen next*? as you write, make sure your characters prepare the ground for the happening, work up to it, dread it or fear it, look forward to it, can't wait for it to come. And as they reveal their reactions in their own various ways, or even go about their everyday business quite unaware that the happening is going to happen, your graph

43

mounts, the screw tightens just that little bit, the audience leans forward, holding its breath – !

Until the final conflicts are resolved and everyone is free to heave a deep sigh and relax and join in the shouts for 'Author!' Which is, of course, *your* cue!

Viewpoint

Just as, when reading a novel, you can usually gather fairly soon who the hero and the heroine are, or that the story is going to be told from the point of view of the hard-working police as they relentlessly hunt down the (as yet) unidentified murderer, the playwright needs to indicate reasonably clearly to the audience whose side they are supposed to be on as they watch his play unfolding. This is particularly important in view of the fact that conflict between the characters will probably mean that they disagree with each other, or have different opinions on what is happening or is about to happen.

As an example of this, I will tell you of an awful error I made when I wrote a play about the assistant to the manager of a small business who devised a cunning method of driving his boss to suicide. The boss, who was proud of the fact that though small, his firm remained independent, was conned into believing that, first, his wife had inexplicably walked out on him; second, his bank manager had refused to grant the loan he'd been counting on; third, some shares he'd been advised to invest heavily in had fallen drastically in value with the result that he'd lost all his money. As everything apparently disintegrated around him, the poor man dazedly took the only way he felt he had left and threw himself out of the window, leaving his assistant free to phone triumphantly and tell the wife (now the widow) with whom he had been having a secret affair, that they were free to be together at last, and that once they could go ahead and sell out to a much bigger company, whose offers the boss had been steadfastly refusing, they could really start living high. By an accident with the switchboard, the call was overheard by the third character in the play, the boss's faithful secretary, who was able to reveal all to the police.

The plot itself was not too bad, but I never made it clear as I wrote the play whether the audience should be desperately hoping that Tim, the assistant, would get away with his daring crime, or whether they should have been rooting for poor Mr Hathaway, with the result that when the play was performed, the audience didn't get a great deal out of it, but I learned a valuable lesson as I watched their slightly bewildered reactions to what was taking place on the stage, and noted the air of relief that prompted the polite applause when the curtain fell. It was not particularly gratifying to realise I had made a terrible mistake, but at least, since I had watched the play myself and been able to recognise what was wrong, that's one mistake I will never make again.

And neither need you. Always be quite sure in your own mind where the sympathy of your audience should be, and which character or characters they should be identifying with.

In a one-act play, the audience will generally begin to identify with whichever characters they meet at the opening of the play, unless it is clear from what those characters say to each other that they are obviously 'baddies' or that they are merely hanging around waiting for the really important personage or personages to appear. But in a one-act play, there isn't enough time to 'prepare the ground' at any great length for the entrances of the main characters. You should begin to start the action, reveal the Question, introduce your main characters, as near the first page of the script as you can.

If the curtain rises on two press photographers with cameras who are waiting at an airport for the arrival of a VIP – a film star or politician – and the VIP does not actually appear until, say, half-way through the play, then your main characters here have got to be the press men (or women) rather than the apparently more important person who comes in later. The audience will have got to know the two photographers, will have begun to identify with them and their problems (which will, of course, provide the Question) and if you switch half-way through to some different Question involving the VIP, this will throw the whole play out of balance.

In a full-length play, it is far more usual to open the first Act with minor characters who refer to the principal actors and talk about their activities or personalities. The audience does not expect here that they will meet the hero or the heroine immediately, they are quite happy to wait and let their curiosity and interest become aroused.

Look at any good one-act play and you will see that generally, the main characters with whom the audience must identify and sympathise, appear if not on the first page, then certainly within the first two or three. But in full-length plays, the first few pages are almost always some sort of 'build-up' for the entry of the principal characters later.

In *When We Are Married*, the celebrants of their Silver Wedding are off-stage when the play opens, and are discussed by the maid, the young organist who is about to be dismissed, and the 'help'.

In *Macbeth*, the Witches, who open the play, ominously mention their forthcoming meeting with Macbeth, and Macbeth himself does not appear until Scene III.

Joan in Shaw's *Saint Joan* does not enter until Robert de Baudricourt and his Steward have had an argument about why the hens are not laying, and the Steward has tried to protest that so long as Robert will not see the Maid, who is trying to obtain an audience with him, there will be no eggs.

It is also a good general rule that your Question will be concerned with the efforts of *the characters the audience must identify with* to overcome their difficulties, find the

46

answer to their problem or escape some threatened fate. There are exceptions, of course; in Emlyn Williams' *Night Must Fall*, the main character is a murderer and therefore cannot be 'sympathetic' morally from the point of view of the audience. Here, though the Question still concerns the main character, Danny, but from a sort of 'back-to-front' angle – the audience is not biting its nails wondering if he'll manage to get away with the murder that seems inevitable, but feverishly wondering whether someone will manage to stop him before it's too late.

Do not attempt something as complicated as this in your first play, though. Keep to a sympathetic character or group of characters of whom the audience can whole-heartedly approve, and make sure he, she or they not only gain the support of your audience but keep it (and play on it, thus building up your graph) all through the action until the final curtain.

Chapter Five

DIALOGUE

When you settle down to begin your play, clothing your skeleton – plot – with the words which will make your characters live and persuade your audience that they are real, the first thing to bear in mind is that the 'dialogue' which will fill up the pages of your blueprint is completely different from any other type of writing. There can be no play without words; it would turn into something else – a mime or a dance-drama. The very word 'audience' comes from the Latin verb 'audire', meaning 'to hear'. So however wonderful your plot, however important you think the visual aspect of the play should be, never lose sight of the fact that it is primarily with the words you give your characters to speak that you will create your play.

This phrase 'the words you give your characters to speak', is very important, for every word of dialogue in your play must be written with the awareness that, when the play comes to life on the stage, each word will be *spoken*. Your play should not be written to be read by the eye: it is not a narrative, it is not a letter, a report, a newspaper article – it is, in fact, unique, for there is no other art form which consists entirely of words intended to be spoken by imaginary characters.

The main point to remember with regard to dialogue, then, is that this is no place for 'literary' writing. 'Literary' writing is not the same thing as good writing; you may think of a brilliant play, but if it is set in a slum – or a prison – or even a pub – the characters will not sound at all convincing if they address each other in flawless BBC English, or as though they were Professors of Literature conversing over afternoon tea.

Your skill as a playwright will show not in the wonderful way you balance phrases, or where you put your commas and full stops, or even in the fact that you follow all the rules of grammar and never split infinitives. The playwright's task is to give immediacy, impact and conviction to these all-important words which make up the dialogue, the words the characters will speak. In a play, there may be broken sentences, interruptions from another character, wrong use of grammar. However, this must not be because you, the playwright, don't know any better, but because your *character* has had no education, and that is the way *he* would talk.

Writing a play poses a thrilling challenge. We don't describe a scene or a situation in the way the author of a novel might do, we take our audience with us so that they *live through the experience itself*; they hear what was actually said at the time, they are there as everything happens!

In spite of the proverb that actions speak louder than words, we rarely reveal our innermost selves in what we do. It is when we open our mouths to speak that we give ourselves away. Even if what we say is a lie, that lie will speak volumes. We are what we say, and your characters will exist and live in the lines you create for them.

Every person in the play (even though they all spring, of course, from your own mind, since you are the author) will speak in a subtly different way because every one of them is an individual and a 'character' in his or her own right.

If you take this to extremes, you will produce dialogue peppered with verbal mannerisms of the cliché sort, such as:

'I say, old chap, got a tenner to lend me? Came out without the jolly old wallet, don't you know, haven't got a bean!'

How many people do you know who actually talk like

49

that? It's familiar enough because this sort of character was used a lot in plays of the Twenties and Thirties, when the 'upper class idiot' of the period actually did exist. Another very popular character of those days was the dim-witted, adenoidal maid, whose lines consisted mainly of 'Yes, mum' and a lot of sniffing.

But remember that even the traditional methods of communication in say, the upper middle class circles of twenty years ago, have altered drastically, and since you are writing your play *now*, you will 'date' it if you employ slang or phrases you recall from your own childhood. And you will also get into deep water if you set your play among people in a section of the populace with which you yourself are not familiar. Do you know how an Archbishop talks in private life? Or a middle-eastern oil magnate? Or a London taxi-driver?

As a playwright, it is your duty to begin right from this minute to open your ears and start listening to the way people talk to each other in as many different environments as you can. What people say to each other is the raw material from which you will shape and select the sort of dialogue you will need to use in your play. Nobody can write a play successfully if they aren't interested in what others say, how they put their feelings over to their listeners, the way they respond to questions. Even if your play is only a modest one set among the sort of people you know well, continue to listen wherever you go. The use of clichés, speech patterns, the way people employ pauses – it's a fascinating study, and for any writer of a play, just as necessary as the long hours spent working out the intricacies of your plot.

Sounding Real

Unless you are intending to write your play in verse or some other stylized form, you will want the things your characters say to sound real and believable. The things they say must give the impression that it was a spur-of-the-moment thought which came into their heads and prompted their remarks, not as though they knew days ago what they were going to say or are quoting from some sort of prepared speech.

You have to remember that, as the play progresses, each incident, each small development of the action, is taking place – or at least, so it should seem to the audience – for the first time, everything is fresh and so the reactions of the characters must sound spontaneous. Often the main thing wrong with a play is the fact that all the dialogue is written in stilted language, which takes away the effect of immediacy, and makes the characters sound as though they've been robbed of the last little drop of human feeling, and are mechanical toys which the author has wound up and thrust onto the stage, in order for them to simply 'go through the motions' of seeming to be real.

Here is an example of the sort of stilted dialogue I mean:

ROY: So we have been left alone at last, Annabel, though I fear Father was reluctant to withdraw into the library.

ANNABEL: I too noticed his disapproving frown. But surely, my dear Roy, he cannot help but be aware that we love each other, and that you brought me here this evening with the intention of asking me to become your wife?

ROY: Then – Annabel! You realised what my invitation signified? Oh, give me your answer, my darling, I can wait no longer.

ANNABEL: It is yes, as you knew very well that it would be.

ROY: Annabel!

(They embrace)

If spoken by two people on a stage, this would sound utterly unreal. There would be no urgency in the lines, no sense that we were watching a scene between two live characters. This is one extreme, language which is too contrived to be believable.

At the other extreme, we will see what might actually result if, in your enthusiasm to capture 'real-life' dialogue, you listened in with a tape recorder to two new-comers, say, entering a restaurant. On your tape, you might record the following:

'Here?'
'Yeah, OK.'
(Rustling, movement etc.)
'Quite nice, isn't it?'
'Only been open a couple of weeks. I came in with Bob the other day – Tuesday – no, it would have been Wednesday, it was that day we had the row in work, oh Gawd, Bob said – '
'What you having, then?'
'Let's have a look.'
(Pause, rustling, movement, etc.)
'What d'you think grouse tastes like?'
'Don't have grouse.'
'What *you* having?'
(Pause)
'I'm hungry.'
(Pause)
'Curtains are nice. It's quite nice really, isn't it?'
'I fancy trout.'
(Pause)
'Did you ask her?'
'Yeah. She said it's OK.'
'The waiter looks like he's coming.'
(Rustlings, movement, etc.)
'Two steaks, please. And – d'you want soup or fruit juice?'

In actual fact, what you'd have on your tape would probably be much less orderly than the scrappy bits of conversation I have detailed above. You will find, if you ever do record two people talking in real life without their knowledge, that the result is a jumble of grunts and mumbles, long pauses, throat clearing, half-finished remarks, repetition, side-tracking and general vagueness.

The main points I want to make about this sort of 'real life' dialogue are that firstly, nothing of any significance has been said by the couple in the restaurant, so (bearing in mind that every word in a play has to count and pull its weight) none of this would be the slightest bit useful to a playwright; secondly, this sort of rambling is excruciatingly boring to listen to, and you must at all costs avoid letting your audience become bored.

If ever you feel tempted to transfer 'real' dialogue into your play, thinking that this will be certain to add authenticity, avoid the temptation, even if it seemed an absolute gem of eternal truth and meaning at the time. For just as the framework of your play must be artificially constructed, bearing little relation to what actually happens in real life, so the dialogue too is – however 'real' it may sound – necessarily an artificial form of writing, requiring skill and technique and again, an understanding of what you are doing, and why.

All dialogue in a play should help to fulfil one of two purposes: it should assist in clarification and development of the action, or it should in some way express character in a meaningful manner. Sometimes, dialogue does both at the same time. But as with Time and Place, the playwright is restricted by the form in which his blueprint has to be written. I have already pointed out that a playwright is never allowed to explain anything, so all the things that might, in some other type of writing, be narrated – the scene, the events that are going on, the feelings and reactions of the characters, what they think – have to be clearly expressed through the single medium of *words for the characters to say*.

Therefore the playwright's task is to balance the actual putting across of anything relevant to the plot or to what sort of people the characters are, with the impression that what they say as the play progresses is the result of spontaneous thought. Since this is something we never have to do in real life – invent words for other people to say which will fulfil at least one of the two purposes I have mentioned above – it is bound to appear strange at first, and may need some getting used to. Writing dialogue is possibly one of the most skilled forms of literary craftsmanship there is.

As with the construction of your plot, you will need to select from the masses of everyday things people say as they talk around you wherever you go, and choose words and phrases which will make the speeches you give your characters seem real and alive. But a discussion that might take an hour in real life, with all the turns and ramblings the conversation would follow, has to be boiled down to essentials in a play. Remember, you have to work through your whole plot in half-an-hour for a one-act play, or two hours for a full-length one. Your dialogue has to be sharp and meaningfully written, and you need to be aware exactly why each speech has been included, instead of just writing vaguely a lot of lines that seem to 'sound nice'.

If one of your characters is a poet who insists on rambling at great length about the effect of moonlight, or how lovely the trees look in their spring green, or even the beautiful hair of one of the other characters, then obviously, you must allow him to ramble to a certain degree, or else the audience will not get the full impression of his character. The same with, say, an elderly lady who is for ever bemoaning the fact that 'things weren't like this in my young days', or an ex-soldier who is inclined to bore the other characters with reminiscences of his Army life. Here, the vagueness and seeming irrelevance of what they might say will be included in your dialogue for a purpose – to express character – that is just as necessary as the exposition of the plot, since it makes the protagonists seem real people. But if you find you are including rambling dialogue (or even descriptions of the moonlight or the trees or the characters themselves) without being able to tell yourself why it is there; if, in fact, you were simply 'padding' out your blueprint and filling up space on the pages – then beware. Your audience will probably have already started to yawn, even if they haven't actually fallen asleep or walked out of the auditorium and gone home.

Character in Dialogue

There are two main difficulties which beset the playwright who is attempting dialogue for the first time. They are completely opposed to each other, and whichever one you might find yourself struggling with will depend on the type of person you are and the way you think. One is the temptation to do what I have just mentioned in the last chapter, fill up the pages with a great deal of rambling speech that gives the impression the play is progressing wonderfully well, but if it is boiled down to essentials, really contains nothing of any real import or significance, and so is vague, woolly and consequently boring. The other is to come to a standstill and wonder what on earth Mary and Joan can say to each other for two more pages until it's time for Henry to enter.

We have already seen that all dialogue has to be there for a purpose – either to further the action and the plot, or to express character. But though 'expressing character' may seem to extend mainly to obvious examples I have already given such as the elderly lady yearning for the lost days of her youth, or the Army veteran, even the things that ordinary everyday people say express far more character than one might imagine. If we examine this more closely, you will see how, as well as keeping your dialogue to the point, sharp and relevant, the expression of character will also help you to overcome the paralysing difficulty of trying to spin out a situation and wondering 'What on earth can they say next?' every few lines.

Here is a piece of dialogue between two people:

> JONES: Hello, Bob. Haven't seen you for ages. I hope you're keeping well?
> SMITH: Oh yes, I'm fine, thank you. And you?
> JONES: Very well, thanks. I expect you heard about the merger. I own both the companies now.
> SMITH: Yes, I had heard. Congratulations. I hope it hasn't landed you with too much extra work.
> JONES: Well, as a matter of fact, I've decided to take on a partner, and I was intending to ring you to see whether you'd be interested.
> SMITH: Interested! I'd accept the offer right away.
> JONES: Good. That's settled then. We'll have lunch together and discuss the business side of it.

(They shake hands)

Can you see what is wrong with this? Let's say it's from a play in which the plot is that Smith has some deeply hidden grudge against Jones, and is secretly planning his ruin. This short bit of dialogue will come early in the play where Smith has 'arranged' a casual meeting, fully aware that Jones will ask him to become a partner. Naturally, he intends to accept the offer, since he wants to oust Jones altogether and take over the companies himself.

But this piece is poorly written because although the characters say what we want them to say, and in a reasonably concise manner – not too vague, but not too contrived either – the dialogue is completely lacking in any sense of character.

The main reason why this is so is because Smith and Jones state only *facts*. What each of them says is the absolute truth. They say exactly what is in their minds. Now, no person who is even remotely human ever speaks the absolute truth all the time. And in this case, Smith has an ulterior motive in that, though he pretends to show friendliness and willingness to please, he really hates Jones's guts, so he has an extra good reason for keeping his real feelings to himself.

It is when we stop for a moment and consider not what our characters are going to say but what they *do not under any circumstances want other people to know* – what they are *not* prepared to say – that their particular personalities begin to emerge and colour their speech.

Everyone, every single person in the world, has something, however trivial, that they want to keep secret and would die rather than reveal to others. In a play of action, which does not delve too deeply into the minds and emotions of the characters, the secret will probably be something concrete – Peter and Maria don't want Mother to find out that they are really married; Gerald doesn't want his fiancée to know that his pretty secretary spent the night in his flat; the Chairman is desperately trying to keep the fact that the firm is on the verge of bankruptcy from his creditors – and so far as Smith and Jones are concerned, Smith doesn't want Jones to know that becoming a partner is only the first step in his plan of revenge.

But the secrets that even the most ordinary character keeps locked up in his or her mind are less factual than this, they are the hopes, the fears, the worries and anxieties that are personal to us all in varying degrees and which, expressed through the medium of your dialogue, will make your characters live for us.

A man is secretly – perhaps not even consciously – afraid that people will look down on him because he comes from a humble background and didn't have a good education. Perhaps Jones, even though he has got on in business, is a man like that. How would he speak to people? To Smith, for instance?

We'll re-write that piece of dialogue between them, bearing in mind Mr Jones's sensitivity about his origins and lack of education.

> JONES: Hello, Bob. Haven't seen you for ages. Keeping well?
> SMITH: Oh yes, I'm fine thank you. And you?
> JONES: Not doing so badly, all things considered. Heard about the merger, did you? Both the companies are mine now.
> SMITH: Yes, I had heard. Congratulations. I hope it hasn't landed you with too much extra work.
> JONES: I've always worked hard, Bob, never been afraid of work. But as a matter of fact, I have been thinking about taking on a partner – somebody to handle the more – well, you know, the more social side. Give the old firm a touch of class, that sort of thing. You'd be ideal. I was going to ring you about it, see whether you'd be interested.
> SMITH: Interested! I'd accept the offer right away.
> JONES: You could do a lot worse, you know, even if I say it myself. Well, we'll have lunch together, eh, and sort out the details. I'll get my secretary to ring you.

(They shake hands)

Can you see how this has brought a little depth into the conversation, even though Jones has said nothing directly about his origins or lack of education? In his speeches, we can detect a feeling of justifiable pride that he (the son of a labourer, no less!) has risen to the heights of owning two companies, and that he might not have a string of 'A' Levels but he knows he's got a good head for business and is going to go far. At the same time, the business brain that has stood him in such good stead has recognised that he could do with someone a little more polished to promote the aspects of the firm he himself is too shy and inexperienced

58

to cope with, hence his offer to Smith, though he can't help a touch of condescension creeping into his manner when he makes the offer. Smith, he insinuates, is highly honoured to have been chosen to provide the 'touch of class', since that's about all he has to recommend him, not a capacity for work and keen business sense like Jones himself.

We can take this a step further. Jones has become more of a real person to us, but how about Smith? What is he trying to keep secret? The fact that he feels nothing but contempt for boring old Jones, and that he has negotiated this apparently casual meeting in order to worm his way into the firm and get a foothold so that he can topple Jones from his place at the top? But of course, he can't let Jones have even the slightest inkling of his real intention, though the audience, who are fully aware of his villainous plan and have already cast him as the 'baddie' – the playwright having made sure they regard Mr Jones with sympathy – will be watching with great interest to see how he gets on, and will grasp what he is doing, conning dear old Jones, though his words – on the surface – give nothing away.

So once again, we re-write the dialogue, this time bearing in mind Smith's ulterior motives.

> JONES: Hello, Bob. Haven't seen you for ages. Keeping well?
> SMITH: Yes, I'm fine thanks. Not forging ahead the way you are, though. Congratulations on the merger.
> JONES: Oh, heard about it, did you? Not bad going, all things considered, is it? Both the companies are mine now.
> SMITH: And they couldn't be in better hands. I always said you'd get to the top. Must be an awful lot of work for you, though.
> JONES: I've always worked hard, Bob, never been afraid of work. But as a matter of fact, I have been thinking about taking on a partner – somebody to handle the more – well, you know, the more social

side. Give the old firm a touch of class, that sort of thing. You'd be ideal. I was going to ring you about it, see whether you'd be interested.

SMITH: Well, I'm flattered, of course, but Robbins is retiring and there's a chance of a really big step up for me – managership of the branch in Budapest. Mind you, I've never been too keen on handling one of the overseas branches – too much paperwork and red tape. You get out of contact with the customers. I do prefer the more personal touch, I think people appreciate it.

JONES: My own feelings exactly. The personal touch is everything in business, everything. You know, you're just the man I need, I can't afford to lose you. How about it? I can make you a very good offer.

SMITH: Well, I'm tempted. Very tempted.

JONES: You could do a lot worse, you know, even if I say it myself. I think you'll find the prospects will more than outweigh a managership in Budapest. Look, let's have lunch together and talk it over. I'll get my secretary to ring you this afternoon. I think I'm free Thursday.

SMITH: (smiling) How can I refuse? All right, old pal, it's a deal!

(They shake hands)

You will see that by 'expressing character' – more specifically using what Smith and Jones *do not want found out* to colour what they say – the original piece of dialogue has not only become more real, interesting, bringing in conflict between the two personalities who each have their own reasons to want their own way here, but it has also *doubled its length*, though nothing has been said except exactly what was said the first time.

Most of Smith's new speeches are flattery of Jones, playing on his sensitivity about his background (oh yes, Smith is aware of his 'old pal''s little weakness) or a lie about the opportunity in Budapest, dangled before Jones to make him all the more determined that Smith is the man he wants. We could even take this further and write the scene so that Jones, meeting Smith apparently casually, hadn't yet considered that he needed a partner to provide the 'touch of class'. How might Smith persuade him to do so? Perhaps you'd like to try your own hand at this one.

One point to note is that it is essential, in this story of Smith's take-over bid, that the sympathy of the audience should by this time have been directed towards Jones, so that they are wholly on poor, shy, blustering Mr Jones's side, and feel that Smith is becoming a threat to their hero's security. If the point of view from which the story is going to be told has not been made clear, consider for a moment how easy it would be to confuse and baffle the audience and make them feel unable to participate fully in the play.

Without altering a single word of this piece of dialogue, the playwright could cast Jones as the villain and Smith as the character with whom the audience should sympathise, by revealing not that Smith was trying to get even with Jones because of a grudge, but that Jones's firm was callously planning to raze Smith's dear old mother's house to the ground and rob her of her home in order to build skyscraper flats. Smith, in a desperate attempt to stop this bulldozing, is trying to get into the firm so he can sabotage the deal for the flats. But can he persuade his awful pal to give him a job? Tense moment as he mutters about Budapest. Will Jones rise to the bait? He does, and Smith's smile at the end is not one of triumph, but relief.

If the audience has not already been shown clearly whose side they are supposed to be on, if by this time in the play they don't know who to sympathise with, then the conversation will, apart from confusing them, lose a great deal of its interest and leave them at a loss, so you will see that plot and dialogue have to be interwoven to carry your graph forward as you write your play.

You should note that even though Jones is trying hard to keep his personal secrets from the world, and thinks nobody knows he is sensitive about his background, Smith is not only aware of this, but turns it to his own advantage in the way he manipulates Jones, flatters him and plays up to him. Jones, however, will never realise that his weaknesses might be obvious to others. He will keep trying to hide his secrets until the day he dies, and the fact that he is doing this will colour everything he says, and the way he will behave in any given situation.

It would make things even more complicated if Smith, in his turn, had some sort of hang-up about *his* background, and resented, say, the fact that he'd never been given credit for making his way, because his family name was 'magic' in business, and opened all doors; but since Smith has already got one secret – his ulterior motive for wanting to get into Jones's firm – that is enough to ensure that he will seem reasonably real to an audience. One secret, of whatever sort, is generally – at least when you are beginning to write plays – sufficient for each character, apart from secrets in the plots that they may be trying to cover up.

This marks an important difference between 'real' characters on the stage and real people. In real life, human beings have so many hang-ups and guilt feelings, complexes and neuroses, that they are impossibly complicated and it's a wonder they ever manage to communicate at all, there are so many prejudices and sensitive spots and things they don't want others to know about themselves. Characters on the stage can seem quite real if they have only one personal secret and a lot of human reactions, like becoming upset, frightened or angry. This can be entirely convincing, and is all that is necessary for the moment to give depth to your dialogue.

Really great dramatists, however, become great because

they are able to include many 'secrets' and weaknesses – as well as strengths – in their characters. Take Hamlet, for instance. His feelings towards his dead father, towards his mother, towards his uncle, towards the girl he supposedly loves, are so complex that scholars are still trying to analyse and sum up his personality. Hamlet is ambivalent, vague, he procrastinates, he can't make up his mind, yet his behaviour springs so much from inner problems, worries and torments that he can easily seem more real to an audience than their son-in-law or the boy next door.

Shakespeare has achieved this because he gives us a knowledge of, and insight into, Hamlet's mind that we can never have into the mind of another living human being. We will never really and truly know everything about anyone, but we feel we know Hamlet completely, even though we may not understand him. This again is one of the artificialities of the theatre.

In the sort of plays of relationship which I have suggested you avoid for the time being, as they are so difficult to tackle, much of the action concerns not only the private 'secrets' of the protagonists, but how much of each person's closely-guarded 'secret' is known to the others, and how they all use what they know to try and manipulate others to get their own way, to hurt, to make up for ways in which they feel they have been manipulated themselves. A notable play of this type is Edward Albee's *Who's Afraid Of Virginia Woolf?* in which all the characters become involved in the bizarre 'secret life' of the main protagonists and the playwright details how they manipulate each other through their most desperately vulnerable weaknesses. Wrenching climaxes can be achieved in this sort of play as the characters force each other to bare their souls, or bring an emotional 'victim' face to face with what he has fought so hard to keep from the rest of the world. But if you study *Who's Afraid Of Virginia Woolf?* you will see how difficult and complex such plays are to write.

Blanche in Tennessee Williams' *A Streetcar Named Desire*

63

is another such emotional 'victim' who is brought face to face with the reality she has tried to ignore, and has all her illusions shattered. If you study this play, too, you will see that this type of writing is not for a beginner. Stick to your graph, the posing of your Question, the characters with weaknesses and things to hide, and a plot full of incident.

Nothing But The Truth?

It would be wrong to say that nobody in a play must ever speak the truth at all, but if the playwright is aware that most of his characters have generally got something, however innocent, to keep from the others, this not only gives depth to what they say but helps to keep the tension, the interest, the conflict, piling up so that the audience doesn't have a chance to become bored.

In addition to this, it will sound completely wrong if two characters meeting for the first time follow the procedure of asking each other direct questions, answering them comprehensively and keeping nothing back. People in real life – on which we are basing our dialogue – will rarely take a direct route in communicating with others, and will be reluctant to reveal all even if they have no secrets to hide.

Only in a very bad play will the following kind of dialogue appear:

> ANNE: Hello. Who are you?
> JOHN: My name is John Smith. What's yours?
> ANNE: Anne Brown. Where are you from, and what are you doing here?
> JOHN: I'm a sailor from Liverpool, on leave at the moment. I'm having a holiday here in London. What are *you* doing here?
> ANNE: I live here. I work in an office and I have a small flat in Hampstead.

People in real life may indeed ask questions, but the question might well be evaded or answered by another. For instance, if husband and wife are quarrelling, the following dialogue would sound far more realistic than if they actually answered each other's questions:

> JIM: All right, so what do you think you were playing at tonight?
> ANGELA: Playing at? What about you? How you've got the gall to face me after your disgusting behaviour with that – that tart –
> JIM: Melody happens to be a very intelligent girl as well as being beautiful. Surely even *you* can tell the difference between gentlemanly appreciation of somebody's conversation and – whatever else you had in your dirty mind. Though judging by your taste – Max, for instance, is nothing but a smooth-tongued shark who makes a living at buttering up older women –
> ANGELA: (furious) Are you insinuating that I'm too ancient to attract a man unless he thinks he can get something out of me? Max appreciates mature beauty, not like you – just a baby-snatcher, running after anything that flaunts a mini-skirt at you –
> JIM: Well, let's face it, you haven't got the legs any more, have you?

Often the playwright can use the fact that people will say something quite different to what they actually mean to give character and interest to dialogue. If, for instance, you want to write a play about how Martha, an experienced collector for Worthy Causes, goes about raising money for the Church Organ Fund, the audience will know quite well from the following dialogue that Martha is manipulating the cantankerous Mr Lawford, and will enjoy watching her at work:

MARTHA: (as MR LAWFORD opens the door to her knock) Oh, I – I'm so sorry, I didn't realise –

MR LAWFORD: Didn't realise what?

MARTHA: I mean – I do apologise for troubling you. I thought Mrs Jarvis lived here.

MR LAWFORD: (irritably) Jarvis? There's never been a Jarvis in this house.

MARTHA: No, as soon as you opened the door, I knew I was wrong. I'd never have called if I'd realised this was the Lawford house, I'd have known you wouldn't be interested.

MR LAWFORD: (exasperated) Talk sense, woman. Interested in what?

MARTHA: No, please, I'm awfully sorry. I know you don't go to church.

MR LAWFORD: Ah, the church is begging again, is that what it is? What does it want now? A new roof?

MARTHA: I really am sorry. I'll go –

MR LAWFORD: (nastily) Such a skinflint, am I? The local miser?

MARTHA: (earnestly) Oh, of course not.

MR LAWFORD: Liar! Well, you can prove the village gossip wrong for once. Tell me about this new roof or whatever it is, and I might even be persuaded to make a contribution. (He laughs at his own joke)

MARTHA: Oh, I wouldn't dream of bothering you, Mr Lawford.

MR LAWFORD: (barking) Don't twitter, woman. Are you going to tell me about it or aren't you?

Even details of your characters' personal lives, their opinions and thoughts and feelings, can be held back to be revealed at strategic moments, thus keeping the interest of the audience. The more 'secrets' you, the playwright, can keep in reserve, the more fascinated and curious your audience will become, the more they will want to know everything about your characters.

In some plays – *When We Are Married* is a good example – the 'secret' or half-truth on which attention is being focussed can be a group affair rather than a personal one. Some of the characters may share a conspiracy of silence, keeping something from the others. In this sort of situation, the members of the 'group' will confer with each other and probably tell other characters who are not 'in the know' outright lies to keep their secret. All this makes for undercurrents, subterfuges, awareness that each speech may mean something much deeper than appears on the surface. This unspoken and concealed aspect of the dialogue, the fact that people say one thing and mean another, provides what is sometimes called the 'sub-text' of a play.

The 'sub-text' will of course vary in depth and intensity depending on the nature of the play, but often it will be through what is *not* said, what is held back or evaded or twisted away from, that your characters will achieve much of their 'reality'.

We have already discussed how personal 'secrets' and secrets in the plot can add interest to dialogue, but this new aspect – the evasion, the half-truth, the holding back of some detail – applies particularly to dealing with the emotions of your characters. Two characters who are in love with each other may share a scene where they talk about apparent trivialities – one of the occasions where trivialities are not only permissible but necessary, since the lovers may be too shy to reveal their love for each other, and are therefore obliged to communicate on a superficial level. The audience, who are aware of their feelings, will guess that when Bruce says: 'The moonlight's beautiful tonight' and Monica answers: 'Yes, I love the way it makes the sea look silvery', he is really saying: '*You* are beautiful tonight' and she is responding: 'Yes, everything is perfect because you are with me.' This same method can also be used effectively when two characters hate each other.

Study any good play and you will find scenes where there are cross-purposes, half-truths, evasions, refusals to reveal true feelings, thoughts or emotions. And never feel that if one of your characters asks a question, that question has to be answered. If it is partly answered, evaded or lost because another person on the stage suddenly comes out with something else, that makes for good, realistic and natural-sounding dialogue.

Dialect

Don't write even a 'dialect' play phonetically, leave it to the actors to provide the accents you require. If you are setting the play in Liverpool and you want everyone to speak with a Liverpool accent, give an indication of this on your introductory page where you have listed Characters, Scene and Time, and if the actors can manage a Liverpool accent, they will do the rest. If they aren't skilled enough to be able to speak in Scouse, it doesn't matter what you write phonetically, it still won't sound correct and it will make difficult reading when people are assessing your script.

The best way to set a play in a dialect setting is to use methods of sentence construction and authentic turns of phrase, but write the actual words of the script in reasonably correct English. For instance, if you have a character who is supposed to be Welsh, it will sound much more convincing if the speech you give her reads:

'Nice day it is'

rather than:

'Isn't it a lovely day?'

The same applies to 'foreign' characters. Unless you are actually going to provide them with speeches in their own language, it is better to use speech patterns that a foreigner would use if attempting 'broken English' and to write the words correctly, rather than include monstrosities like:

'But zis is what zey told me at ze bus-station.'

68

It is the rhythm of a sentence that carries conviction, rather than the imposing of a 'written' accent. Try to listen to the way different people talk, to become familiar with speech patterns, so that you can write in correct English but with an authentic ring to the way you phrase the sentences.

Chapter Six

THE CURTAIN RISES

So now we are ready to deal with the actual opening pages of your play. Even before you start page 1 of your script, it is as well to pay some thought to the effect that will be created in, for instance, the programme, as the audience peruses it to see what delights you have in store for them.

I made a terrible mistake in the play I have already mentioned where the deeply laid plans of Tim drove his boss to suicide – in my original script, I called the faithful secretary Miss Peabody, and when the company who were producing it started rehearsals, they asked whether I would mind if they altered her name to Miss Peters. And why? Well, this was supposed to be a drama, but the fact that the earnest, bespectacled secretary was referred to as Miss Peabody kept making all the other members of the cast laugh.

So there's a lesson to be learned here. Make sure your characters have names to suit both the personalities you have given them, and the type of play you are writing. If one of your protagonists is the jovial landlord of an English pub who's practically an institution in the village, it might have a confusing effect if you decide to call him Maximilian von Reinhardt, and if your play is meant to be serious, you might find that the same thing happens as with Miss Peabody if you gave the characters names like Myrtle Snifflewade or Alf Groper! So take care not to plant the wrong impression in the minds of your audience even before the curtain has risen at the beginning of your play.

I have already explained that the setting of the play has to be briefly described on your introductory page where you have listed Characters, Scene and Time. When you actually start page 1, either the beginning of your one-act play or the opening of your first Act, you will need to give details of any necessary items of furniture or props that must be present on the stage at the rise of the curtain. There is no need to make your descriptions long and drawn-out, nor provide a complete picture of the setting in your stage directions.

You will often find, particularly in Acting Editions of West End hits, that every detail of the set that was used in the original production is described, down to staircases, conservatories and the pictures on the wall. But since your play might be performed by several different companies, and their resources will vary, this sort of thing is only a waste of time. The most sensible way is to indicate furniture or props that are necessary to the plot, and leave the designer to fill in the rest. Depending on what he can manage, he will fill in whatever he possibly can to convey a convincing picture of the setting you have indicated.

You might start your first page, then, as follows:

ACT ONE. SCENE ONE
(The curtain rises on the REV. ASHBY's study. His desk with a chair behind it is on the left. A large easy chair on the right. Small table at the back with a pile of battered ledgers on it. Either on a coat-stand or on a peg on the door, hangs a black overcoat and leather jacket. A crash helmet stands near them on the floor. Other furniture as desired.)

If your play is one-act, simply put the title as a heading and leave out references to Acts and Scenes. We will assume that the ledgers on the table, the overcoat, leather jacket and crash helmet, are necessary to the action of the play – the Reverend, for instance, is a motorbike fiend, and the ledgers will come in later when some sort of shady dealings are to be revealed as they are perused. The desk and chairs are not strictly necessary, but since you have to have some sort of picture of the setting in your mind as your characters act out the play, it is quite in order to include them as a guide to the designer. He might, if he has a large stage to fill and a stock of furniture to draw on, make the desk rather elaborate and turn the easy chair into a sofa, and even add a large cabinet filled with leather-bound books, a footstool and a standard lamp. On the other hand, he may be trying to manage on a tiny stage and a plain desk and two chairs (with the small table to take the ledgers) will be all there is room for.

So use your opening stage directions as a guide, which can be altered to suit the requirements of the company. As I have said, you really only need to mention anything relevant to the action of the play.

When you have given your stage directions for the set that will be revealed at the rise of the curtain, you proceed to indicate any characters who are on-stage at the beginning of the play, or describe which characters enter. Your opening lines in this case could be followed, to illustrate both these possibilities, by one of the following:

(MRS ASHBY is sitting on the floor, centre, wearing a black leotard. She is meditating with eyes shut and legs folded under her in the nearest she can get to the lotus position.)

or

(The stage is empty, but immediately, MRS ASHBY enters and sits down in the centre of the floor. She is wearing a black leotard. She tries to fold her legs into the lotus position, closes her· eyes and begins to meditate.)

Having set the scene for the readers of your script, who will transfer it to the stage, you are now ready to let your characters begin to tell the story through their dialogue. In this case, you could proceed, for instance, in either of the following ways:

(A few seconds later, the doorbell rings off.)

MRS ASHBY: (opening her eyes) Damn! (yelling) Shirley, the front door!

(ROBIN enters.)

ROBIN: (excitedly) It's the Bishop, Mum. I saw him getting out of the taxi.
MRS ASHBY: But he's not due until tomorrow.
ROBIN: Well, he's here now.

or

(While she is meditating SHIRLEY enters and furtively rummages in one of the drawers of the desk.)

MRS ASHBY: (without opening her eyes) What are you doing, Shirley?
SHIRLEY: (with a guilty start) Nothing, Mum.
MRS ASHBY: (turning to look at her) If you're looking for that copy of *Emmeline*, or whatever it was, your father's in the shed reading it.
SHIRLEY: (goggling) Reading it? Dad?
MRS ASHBY: He feels it's his duty to be fully conversant with all forms of temptation.
SHIRLEY: So *that*'s why he took it away from me yesterday. I thought he disapproved.
MRS ASHBY: (mildly) Not at all, dear. I expect he'll get a lot out of it.

73

In both these cases, we are straight into two different plots, and the characters are well on their way into setting up the problem or posing the Question, and the audience's interest has been aroused – the Show, as they say, is on the Road.

In a full-length play, you will need to give further descriptions of setting if the scene changes, but keep these brief and practical as I have indicated. Also, if there are two entrances to your 'set', a door to the kitchen, for instance, and a door to a bedroom, make it clear in your opening stage directions where these doors or entrances are; for example:

> (There is a door down right leading to the bedroom, and another door, left, which gives onto the hall and kitchen.)

When this is clear, you can allow yourself to say, as the characters come and go (exit JOAN into the kitchen) or (MARY enters from the hall) instead of having to work out whether they are coming or going from stage right or stage left all the time. But do make certain that you have mentioned all necessary points about the set right at the beginning of the play. As I pointed out at the beginning of this book, your script must be clear and businesslike, a working blueprint so that your ideas can be easily translated into three-dimensional form on the stage.

Checklist

Most of the information you will need about the opening of your play and your early pages has already been mentioned, so here's a quick check through to re-cap and bring everything together, as you start work on your script.

1. Bear in mind the limitations of a stage, and of Time and Place within your play.

2. Don't waste words on a lot of introduction. Get right into the situation you want to present to your audience.

3. Begin from the first page to build up your graph of rising tension, interest and conflict.

4. Introduce the Question or problem as soon as possible and hint at further developments to excite the audience's curiosity.

5. If your play is full-length, introduce secondary Questions to back up the main theme.

6. Right from the start, provide conflict of some sort in the interplay between characters.

7. Indicate as soon as possible where the sympathy of the audience should lie, and which character or characters they should identify with.

8. In a one-act play, start with your main characters at the beginning or as near to the beginning as possible.

9. In a full-length play, let secondary characters prepare the ground for the entrance of the main protagonists.

10. Try to give your characters lines that sound 'real', though bearing in mind that all dialogue must assist in the development of the plot or in establishing the personalities of your characters.

11. Keep at least some 'secrets' in reserve for use later in the play.

12. Remember all the time that you have an audience, and that you must not let them become confused or bored.

Establishing Mood

I'd like you to consider two examples here of openings of plays. This is the first:

> (Cottage kitchen, with nets, oilskins, spinning-wheel, some new boards standing by the wall, etc. CATHLEEN, a girl of about twenty, finishes kneading cake, and puts it down in the pot-oven by the fire;

then wipes her hands, and begins to spin at the wheel.
NORA, a young girl, puts her head in at the door.)

NORA: (in a low voice) Where is she?
CATHLEEN: She's lying down, God help her, and
maybe sleeping, if she's able.

(NORA comes in softly and takes a bundle from under
her shawl.)

CATHLEEN: (spinning the wheel rapidly) What is
it you have?
NORA: The young priest is after bringing them. It's
a shirt and a plain stocking were got off a drowned
man in Donegal. (CATHLEEN stops her wheel with
a sudden movement, and leans out to listen) We're
to find out if it's Michael's they are, some time herself
will be down looking by the sea.
CATHLEEN: How would they be Michael's, Nora?
How would he go the length of that way to the far
north?
NORA: The young priest says he's known the like
of it. 'If it's Michael's they are,' says he, 'you can tell
herself he's got a clean burial, by the grace of God;
and if they're not his, let no one say a word about
them, for she'll be getting her death,' says he, 'with
crying and lamenting.'

This is the second example:

(Morning-room in ALGERNON's flat in Half-Moon
Street. The room is luxuriously and artistically fur-
nished. The sound of a piano is heard in the adjoining
room. LANE is arranging afternoon tea on the table
and, after the music has ceased, ALGERNON enters.)

ALGERNON: Did you hear what I was playing, Lane?

LANE: I didn't think it polite to listen, sir.

ALGERNON: I'm sorry for that, for your sake. I don't play accurately – anyone can play accurately – but I play with wonderful expression. As far as the piano is concerned, sentiment is my forte. I keep science for Life.

LANE: Yes, sir.

ALGERNON: And, speaking of the science of Life, have you got the cucumber sandwiches cut for Lady Bracknell?

LANE: Yes, sir. (Hands them on a salver.)

ALGERNON: (inspects them, takes two, and sits down on the sofa) Oh! . . . by the way, Lane, I see from your book that on Thursday night, when Lord Shoreman and Mr Worthing were dining with me, eight bottles of champagne are entered as having been consumed.

LANE: Yes, sir; eight bottles and a pint.

ALGERNON: Why is it that at a bachelor's establishment the servants invariably drink the champagne? I ask merely for information.

These are the beginnings of a great comedy of style and wit – and a great tragedy. The comedy is, of course, Oscar Wilde's *The Importance Of Being Earnest*, and the tragedy is *Riders To The Sea* by J. M. Synge.

What I want you to note particularly is that there is no possible chance that anyone could confuse these two openings, or mistake the first example for a comedy, or the second for a tragedy. Right from the opening lines, the mood of the play has been established, and the audience is left in no doubt as to whether they should be prepared to laugh and be amused, or to agonise and weep.

Whatever sort of play yours is going to be, make sure that you too establish the mood – light and frivolous, or serious, or deeply tragic – right from your opening page, as, though it is possible to alter the mood of a play in the middle, this can only be done successfully in skilled hands, and should never be attempted by a beginner. You will confuse and probably embarrass your audience if, after they have laughed their heads off for ten minutes at the antics of a comic undertaker, for instance, they suddenly realise that the play is meant to be a tragic drama. You need to provide variety, and can include serious scenes in an amusing play, or lighter moments in a tragedy, but never mislead your audience at the beginning. If they think you are promising them something stark and dramatic, make sure that – though it may have touches of humour or wit – something stark and dramatic is basically what they get. If they settle down in the first few moments to enjoy a rollicking romp, then be certain that – though there might even be some heart-rending scenes from time to time – your play romps right on to the end.

Establish the mood clearly right at the beginning, and even if the intensity of mood varies as the play progresses, keep to the same mood right through, otherwise your play will not work.

Chapter Seven

THE PLOT THICKENS

Although any work of art – including a play – must have a feeling of unity about it, a sort of inevitability which sweeps the onlooker breathlessly forward until the finish, when the spell breaks, nevertheless the playwright hard at work on his or her script will find that the play seems to write itself in sections. The beginning and early pages will probably emerge in a frantic whirl of enthusiasm, a desire to get the idea down on paper, and a sense of delicious anticipation as though attacking the play is similar to setting out as an explorer into uncharted territory. The ending, too, will be written in the knowledge that the task is almost done, the work almost over, the journey into that uncharted land nearly completed, which is bound to bring a heady sense of triumph and relief.

The middle section of your play is where the novelty can wear off, the doubts set in, the threads of your plot become so complicated that you don't think you'll be able to unravel them, the characters seem to 'die' on you. The end, you feel, is miles away – that traveller in uncharted territory can sometimes sit down at this point, contemplate what seems to be an empty water-flask, look round desperately for assistance, find none, and give up hope altogether.

Many plays begun with hopes high and on a wave of enthusiasm end up only half-finished. In a way, this is not really surprising, since the concept of 'beginning, middle and end' or, as it is sometimes referred to, 'introduction, complication and resolution' which marked many of the so-called 'well-made plays' of the Twenties, Thirties and Forties inevitably meant that though the beginning (in other words, the first Act) might have been full of interesting promise and the end (the last Act) have reached a staggering climax, there was a tendency for the second Act – the middle of the play, where complications were supposed to occur – to be rather static and boring, with the playwright relying on technique and tricks to keep the audience's attention and keep the action moving.

If you looked at your play from the viewpoints of 'beginning, middle and end', you might find the same sticky sogginess in the central section of your script, the same thinness of invention, the same feeling that it was only with the greatest difficulty that you'd managed to scramble through the awkward central part to get on to that wonderful build-up towards the climax at the end.

That is why I have suggested instead that the play, whether one-act or full-length, is viewed as a rising graph or a working out, right from the first pages, of the Question (or Questions) you have posed to grip and fascinate the audience's curiosity and attention. Don't consider that your play has a 'middle' and that it's something to fill in the gap between the beginning and the end – though this may in fact be true. Regard it as a progression varying in pace from page 1 until you can bring down the final curtain; to a certain extent a journey into the unknown, but one where, unlike the explorer with his empty water-flask, you have taken the trouble, before you set out, to equip yourself with stores and also to fashion a map of sorts. Your carefully planned graph and the basic carpentry you will have done on structure, plot, the manner in which 'secrets' are to be revealed, tension is to be created, the screw tightened with each climax, the audience kept amused, intrigued, *in your power* – all this basic work will ensure that you never lose control of your play or suddenly become 'written out' and have to sit down and wait for further inspiration.

A lot of what goes into any form of good writing, whether a play, a novel or non-fiction, springs from the subconscious, and if you suddenly see everything from a completely different angle, and realise that it works far better than your original plan, this is probably your subconscious handing you a gift – don't ignore it. But, however intuitively you create in a play, because it is necessarily so restricted to the limitations of a stage and has to take technical considerations into account, you *must* do your planning – what I have called your carpentry – before you start to write. And this will mean that, fore-armed with your graph and your plans, you won't find it awkward to scramble through the central section of your blueprint; you'll be aware that all this is laying the ground, advancing your plot, progressing satisfactorily in the way you intended it should, to the nail-biting, nerve-shattering final moments before you ring down the curtain on your thrilled and mesmerised audience, and allow them to recover from the spell.

All the same, since, as I pointed out earlier, it may take you half-an-hour to complete one A4 page, which the actors will sail through in two minutes, you might very well find after the early euphoria has worn off that the actual writing of the script can be hard work, so I am going to mention a few useful hints which could help you over a hurdle, or at least give you some assistance when you think the water-flask has dried up.

Useful Technical Tricks

1. Although Narrators or Prologues are not normally used these days, there is no reason why you should not employ a character – or characters – who will act as a sort of go-between for the players and the audience, if you think you would be able to put your play over better this way. The fact that he or she can speak directly to the audience will give you a rest for a moment from the pressure of having

to invent dialogue which the characters must say to each other, and so long as the Narrator or whoever it is does not keep popping on and off the stage all the time, turning the play into a sort of glorified lecture or monologue, the audience might find this rather refreshing.

The Common Man in Robert Bolt's *A Man For All Seasons* communicates very effectively with the audience, and his appearances are woven in a masterly fashion into the structure of the play.

Alternatively, by incorporating a sort of spoken narrative in what would be called a 'voice over' – pre-recorded and played separately from what the actors and actresses say on the. stage – you can give unity and a framework to your play, especially if it is a full-length one.

This type of linking passage was used to brilliant effect in the dramatisation of *The Diary of Anne Frank*, by Francis Goodrich and Albert Hackett, where extracts were taken from the original text of Anne's diary. Another example is *I Capture The Castle* by Dodie Smith, where the narrative was from the 'diary' of the young heroine of the play.

2. Another way of using a direct link with the audience is to allow the characters, as soon as they walk onto the stage, to notice their onlookers. They may be rather surprised to see their watchers, but should be far more concerned about their own problems to spare more than a brief word before ignoring the audience and getting on with whatever problem needs to be overcome. Occasionally, they might recollect rather guiltily that they have an audience, and one character might say:

'I really think we should explain about John, or they' (nodding into the auditorium) 'won't realise just how difficult the situation is going to be when he arrives.'

A second character might reply:

'Oh, Rob, we haven't got time to explain now. I've got

to fetch some more food – you know John, always ravenous – so I'm going to nip out to the shop. You have a word with Fiona. Try to get it into her bird-brain that she musn't breathe a single thing about the Sale while John's here.'

'Oh, Lord! If he hears about that Sale!' agrees the first character, diverted from thinking about explanations to the audience, and he's back in the play once again.

In this sort of situation, the one thing you must never do is allow the characters to explain anything. They may drop hints or attempt to begin an explanation, but must always be prevented by actual happenings within the play itself, so that they are distracted and forget that the audience is there.

There is no need to worry about accounting for how or why the audience just happens to be present when the plot involves revelations at the Rectory about the Rev. Ashby being the author of that naughty book he had confiscated from daughter Shirley. If the characters simply tell each other in a resigned manner: 'Oh, they're the audience', we can assume that the rest of the protagonists will accept the presence of an audience to be perfectly feasible and reasonable. Some of the characters may even say things like: 'Well, whoever they are, I hope they're going to behave themselves' or 'Oh, how do you *do*? Delighted to meet you, I'm sure', comments that can be tailored to reveal just what type of person that character is, and how they might react under other circumstances.

3. A useful method of assisting your plot onwards is to arrange things at the initial planning stage so that your characters do not enter all at once. String their entrances, throughout the play. One might be on-stage when the curtain rises. A second enters – a short while later, a third appears. After some time, a fourth joins them. Then a fifth. Up to as many as the play will take.

This, of course, would not do for all types of plot, but it is surprising how many situations you could work it into. The members of the group that slowly forms might be relatives arriving one by one – or in couples – at some sort of family gathering; climbers arriving at a hut in the mountains; refugees; survivors from a disaster.

The characters the audience meets first (if this is a one-act play) must be the ones whose side they will take, the sympathetic characters with whom they will identify, if we follow our rules. In a full-length play, you could use this device only in the first Act, certainly not throughout two or three separate acts – but you could pave the way for the entrance of your main character in the conversation of the lesser mortals as they gather and begin to discuss the person (or people) whom they are expecting.

I have previously pointed out that the entrance of new characters does not mark a climax in the play, but this method can be helpful to a beginner because the appearance of a fresh face, with all the interesting possibilities that open up, can act as a tonic if you feel your plot is becoming slightly jaded. If your characters seem to have become boring and you're having a bit of an uphill slog with them, the entrance of somebody new can give a shift in outlook, or create new conflict. The existing group may not want the new character to join them, for instance; or the newcomer might have important news or information which will assist your plot and give the story a twist. Do not just keep bringing people on for the sake of it, though. Remember, everybody in a play has to have some reason – a valid reason – for being on the stage and in the list you have made of your characters.

4. Like all rules, the statement I have just made has its exceptions, and one of them is that if you were writing a play that covered a wide span of Time and Place – like, for instance, *The Story of Mary, Queen of Scots* – you would find it difficult to cope with large numbers of short scenes that ranged from Scotland to France to England and back to Scotland again, over several years. In such a case, particularly if the story of the play is set in royal courts, whether they are ancient or modern – you might be telling the dra-

matic story of an emerging Third World nation today, for example – you might find it easier to write the whole play in a simple basic set with no elaborate scenery, and bring on 'supers' or 'extras' who don't really take part in the action, but who can 'dress' the stage. Shakespeare, whose stage was rather limited so far as difficult scene changes went, employed this method to perfection when he was writing his historical plays. Look at Act I Scene I of *King Henry The Sixth*. The scene setting Shakespeare has given is: 'Westminster Abbey' – but since Act I Scene II is going to take place in France, before Orleans, and Scene III in London, before the Tower, it's obvious that no attempt can be made to open Scene I on a grand and realistic set representing the Abbey.

You could perform a play like this with no scenery at all (or hardly any) and each different scene would be indicated and 'dressed' by the 'extras' who accompanied the main protagonists when they entered and left the stage. In Scene I, the crowd which is going to supply the sombre note of an Abbey funeral – that of Henry V – is listed by Shakespeare as: ' . . . the DUKE OF BEDFORD, Regent of France; the DUKE OF GLOSTER, Protector; the DUKE OF EXETER, the EARL OF WARWICK, the BISHOP OF WINCHESTER, HERALDS, ETC.'

These royal and saintly characters do have speaking roles in the play, but the heralds and the 'etc' do not. However, if each time the scene returns to the formality of the English court and its affairs, various similar 'extras' and 'etcs' are included, Shakespeare can change the scenes quickly and range as widely as he likes, using the same method for the different armies; the main protagonists when the French army appears are the Dauphin of France, and the Dukes of Alencon and Reignier, but they are accompanied by 'drum and SOLDIERS'.

A few 'extras' carrying banners, or other significant props, can 'dress' the stage very satisfactorily if you want to cover widely varying scene settings and include perhaps ten different Scenes within an Act – and you can forget about trying to cope with changing scenery. Such 'extras' can also provide atmosphere for a scene that might otherwise be difficult to include in your play – the setting of a fun-fair, a circus, or something like this that would be impossible to transfer satisfactorily onto a stage. And if the producer decided he didn't need the 'extras', he would not bother to use them. It does, however, give you quite a lot of freedom if you want to use this method to try and by-pass the restrictions of the stage somewhat.

5. Yet another method of encompassing widely-ranging and far-flung stories into a single play is to set the scene on 'A Stage' and possibly even allow characters like the producer and stage manager to appear, in between 'scenes' which involve the actual characters in the story, whoever they are to be.

I employed this device in my first successful one-act stage play *Percival, The Performing Pig*, where not only the Producer and Stage Manager (not the real ones, of course) were included in the cast list, but also various spare characters who were brought on, wearing ordinary clothes, and told to 'be' The Scenery, since the real scenery hadn't arrived. In the course of the play, there were about five different changes of scene, but as the setting was a stage where the production team were trying to improvise by, for instance, telling The Scenery to 'put your arms on each other's shoulders, and you can be the farmhouse' or 'stand there and be the weeping willow tree', and the characters in each scene wandered on and off as the Producer yelled for them, changes of scene proved no trouble, and the rather rambling tale of the adventures of Percival the pig, his wonderful operatic voice, his debut on the London stage and his eventual triumphant return home to the farm, were brought into a framework of half-an-hour on a stage, where the team had to get their play on somehow, in spite of their scenery being so disastrously missing.

Plays have been set on stages during rehearsals, where

the audience are given a thrilling glimpse of the 'real' world of the theatre – one well-known one-act play along these lines was Maurice Baring's *The Rehearsal*, at which the original cast, including The Author, were rehearsing *Macbeth* on the stage of the Globe Theatre for the first performance. This type of play is usually a comedy, as we see everything going crazily wrong. A modern example employing a similar device is *Noises Off* by Michael Frayn, and, in contrast, Graham Holliday's *The Scottish Play* (both published by Samuel French) which again deals with a production of *Macbeth*, but this time in a tragic rather than a comic manner.

You will see that by using 'A STAGE' as your setting, you can give yourself quite a lot of scope, but naturally, if you yourself aren't very familiar with amateur acting (or, of course, professional acting) you won't be able to give an authentic flavour to your script, so avoid rehearsal and stage settings.

Pace, Tension and Atmosphere

We have already seen that the mood of the play must be clearly established right at the beginning, though as the play develops, you will need to use variety of pace, depth of tension and atmosphere to save the audience from becoming bored. Anything that progresses at exactly the same intensity from beginning to end, with no change of mood, lighter (or darker) moments, without those small climaxes releasing tension before it begins to build up again, anything which is in the nature of a speaker talking in exactly the same tone of voice with no emphasis, no variation of pitch, will send your audience to sleep.

The pace of a play – or a novel, or whatever – means the speed with which events happen. *Waiting For Godot*, for instance, is not a fast-moving play when compared to a French farce, where the characters keep rushing in and out of doors, doing things, trying to avoid each other, keeping on the move. But even in a fast-moving play, you have to have moments of calm, where the players and the audience can catch their breath, as it were.

Also, you have to build up tension, atmosphere and pace so that events which the audience would not have accepted right at the beginning seem to be perfectly natural to them, and can be believed and appreciated if they happen later in the play.

Take the following scene, for instance. A Nurse is sitting at a desk with a night-light, obviously on night duty; the ward is quiet. Suddenly a man in purple pyjamas rushes in wielding a long glittering kitchen knife; 'I'll kill you,' he shrieks; the Nurse grapples with him, he stabs her and she collapses, moaning. He dashes off brandishing his knife.

If a play opened on this scene, it would probably make the audience laugh, because of the apparent ridiculousness of the situation. A killer with a knife (especially in purple pyjamas) is not the sort of thing we encounter every day, and unless the ground has been prepared in advance, any audience will laugh if they are confronted by something unexpected. This is one of the rules of comedy – it has to be something that takes the audience off their guard, catches them unaware. Predictability is rarely funny – or, if it is, it has a humour of its own, which is not what I am talking about here.

In the same way as the purple-pyjama'd killer, the ending of a play like *Hamlet*, where practically all the cast expire one after the other, can seem funny if the audience hasn't become so involved that, to them, it is tragic. No producer would choose to present the last Act of *Hamlet* as an example of tragic drama – if performed without the 'building-up' of tension and atmosphere, the end of the play would seem absurd.

If you have a scene somewhere in your play where the maniac with the purple pyjamas is going to try and kill the Nurse in order to make his escape from the hospital where he has been confined, and then seek out the girl who (he thinks) has betrayed him in order to murder her, this can actually work, but as I have said, you have to build up tension and atmosphere first, and make sure the pace of the play is right. A thriller like this has to start slowly. The pace has to speed up bit by bit. Hints are dropped – indications that something is wrong – people begin to get frightened. The audience, identifying with this general feeling of unease, accepts the situation.

In the case of your maniac killer, you would have to show him (in his purple pyjamas) apparently behaving quite reasonably in the hospital, sitting reading a paper, or being interviewed by a doctor while he sat up in a bed. He would seem to reply in a reasonable manner, yet the doctor might say afterwards, in another scene, that he wasn't quite satisfied with the replies the patient gave to his questions. On this ominous note, the doctor might leave the subject and prepare to welcome the girl who is later going to be the killer's victim to his office. The girl (the patient's adopted daughter, perhaps, or step-daughter?) might, after enquiring about the patient's health, hesitantly ask for advice. She has found some papers in a drawer in the library – or wherever you like to specify – which seem to be connected with an unsolved murder in the area ten years ago. Drop a few more hints as to why she should feel uneasy, or that dirty deeds are about to be afoot, and then build up to your climax, maybe closing your first Act. The girl is reassured by the doctor, the hospital settles down for the night – the audience, however, aware that the girl will be on her own in the family home not very far away – the Night Nurse takes her place at the desk with just the night-light illuminating the stage. The doctor briefly appears to make sure all is well and the patients – especially the one the audience is concerned with – are asleep. The Nurse is left alone again. A clock strikes. Curtains billow in the wind. The Nurse rises, shuts the window, sits down again. And then, as the audience can stand it no longer, on comes the purple pyjama'd killer with his kitchen knife, and far from laughing, the audience will be gripped by the drama of the scene. As the Nurse lies moaning, trying to reach the bell on her desk, and the killer disappears into the night, the curtain falls on Act One, and the audience will be waiting eagerly to see what will happen when it rises on Act Two, which is set in the family mansion where the heroine is alone with just those papers about the unsolved murder to keep her company.

Many inexperienced playwrights can spoil their dramatic climaxes by including too much dialogue. In any scene of deep emotion or violent action – such as this one – or, say, people saying goodbye for what they know is the last time; the 'saved' heroine clinging to the hero who has rescued her; a mother receiving news that her child is dead – anything of this nature – a good rule for writing is: *Don't!*

Rather than have the killer shrieking as he attacks the Nurse, a silent approach would be better and more effective. People saying goodbye for the last time will move the audience to far more tears if they simply clasp hands wordlessly, since mere words will not express what they want to say. The 'saved heroine' spoils the whole effect if she gasps out: 'Oh, Max, thank goodness you came! I – I thought I was – '

Few playwrights can convincingly put into words extreme depths of emotion, and at this stage it is better not to try. Whatever you come up with will sound melodramatic, and might have a drastic effect on the whole climax, especially sentences such as:

'So it was you, was it, you villain?'
'Dead? He's dead? No, I can't believe it – I won't!'
'Tell me it's not true!'
'What are you trying to say?'

All these and many other clichés which are often used to express deep feeling are so well-worn and hackneyed that even if the audience was about to weep, it would probably change its mind. The less you allow your characters to say when under the grip of strong emotion, the better.

In some full-length plays, the playwright has made an attempt to keep the tension at full stretch and the pace from flagging by allowing the curtain to fall on a dramatic climax, and then ringing it up for the next Scene or Act on exactly the same scene, which proceeds to pick up where it left off, with no time lapse in between. An example of this can be found in *Wait Until Dark* by Frederick Knott, between Act Two, Scene Two, and the rise of the curtain on the next scene. The blind heroine has been cornered by the villains, who order her in no uncertain terms to spill the beans and reveal all. The curtain falls on this moment of tension – and rises again on the same moment.

Somehow, this method of running the acts together rarely seems to work successfully, probably because a full-length play should, as we have seen, be constructed differently from a one-act play, even if that one act lasts for two hours. In spite of the fact that the same thread of tension is picked up again if the curtain rises on the last moment of the previous Act or Scene, the fact that there has been an interval has distanced the audience from the action, and the climax of that last scene will have gone stale by the time the curtain rises on it again. This is not, therefore, a good way to start off a Second Act or a Third Act, which should begin to intrigue the audience afresh rather than follow the same well-worn path you have already trodden in the previous Act.

This kind of 'cliff-hanger' had to be used when a serial for films or TV, consisting of several episodes, was concerned, but it is not a good method for building up tension on the stage. For one thing, if you start off an Act with what was previously the high point of the action – the climax – you're going to have to pile on the agony to top it when your Second Act ends. And if you start the Third Act with the dramatic climax of the finale of Act Two, how on earth can you hope to reach a really thrilling finish as the whole play explodes round your stunned audience?

All the best moments of high drama are built up to, worked for, rather than thrown casually away early on in a play. Keep that screw tightening all the time, never throw anything away, hold back your 'secrets', your climaxes, and whatever you *do* choose to reveal to your audience will be all the more effective.

Chapter Eight

THE FINAL CURTAIN

Having worked hard to get your play started, having determinedly plodded through that awkward central section, you
might well heave a sigh of relief as the final curtain begins
to loom and think that the hard graft is over now, the ending
will sort itself out easily. In fact, though, the last part of
a play is probably trickier than the opening. Endings are
notoriously difficult to write successfully, probably because
in real life, there are no 'endings' as such and so the ending
of any work of art, whether play or novel, has to be something which is artificial, but will seem real and convincing
to the audience.

Don't try to struggle to the end of your play if you feel
desperate for a rest. Take a break and then tackle the
ending, which is, after all, the last part of the play the
audience will see, and so contains the last impact it will
make on them; try to start fresh, when you feel able to cope
with all the important points that are involved in the leading
up to that 'final curtain'.

As with the central section, the ending will be far easier
if your preparation before you started writing the play has
been carefully and thoroughly done. The Questions will
have been posed and pondered, secrets guessed-at, problems faced, and your graph will have travelled through its
various developments nearing the final climax and resolution. You should, before you start the play, have some
idea how it is going to end, even if you have not worked

out all the details, and certainly anything that is very complicated, like the fact that the hero was travelling by rail across Siberia when the murder was committed, and his travelling times and connections did not coincide so that it would have been impossible for him to have been at the Rectory, even though Miss Wilder swore she had seen him, and ten other people noticed him walking through the village – this sort of documentation must be carefully planned so that it isn't left to a sudden splurge of detail at the end of the play.

Do not allow all explanations to be made right at the end. Try to space them out a bit, so that part of the Question is explained – a bit more is explained later – and by the time we reach the final climax, all that remains is, perhaps, one important detail. Remember that a play is not like a novel, or even like the blueprint you will be presenting to your interested players. The play, as performed on the stage, passes before the eyes of the audience, and what has happened cannot be recalled. They can't 'stop the play' and go back to Scene II, because they have forgotten exactly what went on between Max and Samantha; or they didn't realise from the conversation in the early part of the play that Mr Roberts's first name (which turns out to be so important) was Tudor.

Anything which the audience should remember must, without actually being rammed down their throats, be made quite clear, so that they don't think in bewilderment: 'I don't remember that!' or 'But what's *he* doing here?' On the other hand, however, a long and involved explanation, whether it comes from one character or is disguised as 'dialogue' and split between the Detective Inspector, his assistant and the hero, can be very boring for the audience and is not the best method of tidying up loose ends at the climax of the play.

Try to give out any necessary explanation in small doses, so that the audience can swallow them without noticing they are there.

94

The Climax of the Play

The climax of your play will be the final 'big moment', the resolution of the Question in whichever way you have chosen to work it out, the release of tension, the letting out of the audience's pent-up breath, the high point on your graph, which then goes into its last downward swing.

A climax does not have to be a scene of dramatic confrontation, nor does it have to contain accusations, raised voices, a lot of noise or violent action. You might, depending on the nature of your play, work up to a climax which could be a single speech or even a moment of complete silence on the stage. Say that your play has been about a young man who turns up at a stately home claiming to be the long-lost heir, and how he fights to prove his identity and claim his inheritance. The climax of the play might come in a single action, where, having discovered that if he is acknowledged as the heir, several people – including the parents of the girl with whom he has now fallen in love – will be ruined, he eventually discovers the vital document he has been looking for to prove his claim, but after standing for a moment in silence, he deliberately, without saying anything, gets out his cigarette lighter and burns the paper, thus relinquishing all hope of proving his real identity. The action of setting light to the paper would in this case be the climax of the play, though the climax would perhaps not be what the audience would have expected. They might have been waiting eagerly for him to find the paper so that he could establish his claim beyond all doubt, but if your Questions – the difficulties that would be faced by all the other people concerned if he was recognised as the heir, and the fact that he had begun to see that love mattered more to him than power, wealth and status – had been propounded successfully, so that we had seen the threads of the problems becoming more involved, had witnessed the development of the hero's character and watched his growing relationship with the girl he loves, then the ending, his rejection of his claim, though he did have a right to it, would be far more satisfactory than his simply finding the paper and everyone having to recognise that he was in fact the real heir.

The audience must always feel that the ending of a play springs directly from the events which have taken place in the earlier part of that play. In Greek drama, it was customary to bring in a character at the end who had little or nothing to do with the events of the play, but who arrived in god-like fashion and sorted everybody out satisfactorily. Since it was always one of the Greek gods, and they arrived on-stage by means of a crane which hoisted them up to give them an appearance of flying down to the level of mere mortals, these characters who tidied up all the ends and finished off the play were known as *deus ex machina* – the god from the machine. Nowadays, though, the audience does not accept the concept of a stranger appearing in the final moments of the play and setting everything to rights. Your climax must be one that has sprung from the Questions and the characters who have held the interest of the audience since the curtain rose, not an imposed 'happy ending' or even 'sad ending' which is provided by a powerful outside person, or even by fate or chance. If the problems of the poor struggling couple, for instance, are all solved in the last moments of the play when a completely new character rushes on-stage waving a cheque and announces that they have won the football pools, this is unlikely to satisfy the audience, especially if it has never been mentioned in the early part of the play that Tom actually did the football pools every week.

If your play has been concerned, however, with the complications arising when the couple *think* they have won the football pools, and begin to start spending the fortune in a startlingly extravagant manner, then discover the coupon never reached its destination, so they are desperately having to try and recover the money – only to discover after further complications that they did win after all – this is quite different, since the advent of a character waving a cheque and announcing their win would be in keeping with the previous action of the play. But a 'surprise ending' which incorporates characters or happenings that seem to have no relevance to the rest of the play will disappoint the audience and leave them feeling thoroughly deflated.

You might, of course, have the person who is going to appear at the end not actually seen beforehand, but if the rest of the characters have been talking about him or her – wondering what he/she will do when he comes, and generally involving him in the action even though he has not yet appeared – if the audience feel that a lot depends on the appearance and behaviour of this mysterious personage, and are waiting with as much interest as the players to see what will happen when he arrives, then his appearance is quite in order, even if it is only a brief one, and comes near the end of the play. Your climax, though, might again be not quite what the audience expects. The climax might be his non-arrival – the fact that the rest of the cast have to carry on without him. *Waiting For Godot* concerns a character who never arrives, but I am thinking here more of a concrete problem confronting the waiting players, who were expecting their important personage to open a fete, say, or lay a foundation-stone. The fact that their guest does not arrive might further the action of the plot by causing hasty changes in the programme to be made – a local person is suddenly recognised as being far more worthy of being given the honour of opening the fete than an 'important personage' who couldn't even be bothered to let them know he wasn't coming. Or else, if your play is a full-length one, somebody is hurriedly disguised and has to play the part of this important character.

Most of these are devices that have been used before – the classic example of the disguised character pretending to be somebody else is *Charley's Aunt* by Brandon Thomas. This was first performed in 1892, however, and as I have pointed out, there is no copyright on a basic situation, and the fun that can arise when somebody is pretending to be somebody else has had many different forms in the theatre since then.

Anti-climax and the 'Wind-down'

The last thing you want is for your play to fizzle into anti-climax so that the audience departs in a grumpy mood, feeling you've somehow cheated them. They expect you to give them a satisfactory climax to your play, to let it happen at the correct moment and for it to give them a feeling that of course, this is exactly the right ending – even if, as I have already mentioned, it might not be entirely the ending they expected.

As you build up to the last big moment, you will feel, as will the audience, that nothing can delay the confrontation, the climax, the revelation, the resolution of all the tangles of the plot, beyond a certain point. Do not keep inventing ways of putting off the big moment if these ways are simply that – pure invention, since there is really no reason at all why the ending should not happen. You may feel you can't let the big scene come yet, or the play will be over too soon; it will be too short; the plot didn't last long enough; the carpentry was all right, but there wasn't enough of it.

If this should happen, it is no good at all to simply delay the ending with cheap tricks. The only way you can make a play which runs out too soon into a longer play is to re-write the whole thing, this time making sure that your carpentry – your Question and the ways in which you will reach its resolution; your graph of mounting climaxes, the 'secrets' you have in reserve and plan to reveal at strategic moments – is sturdy enough to carry you through until the play has developed under its own steam to a more suitable length, so that when the ending comes, it's more or less at the right moment.

People can worry themselves to death about how to make a play last a certain number of pages, or a certain length of time. It doesn't come easily if this is one's first attempt at writing a script. The first time I tried seriously to write a play, I worked out a good plot, planned everything so that entrances and exits were feasible, made sure my characters developed and there was a deep psychological meaning to the action, and started writing. But alas, the 'confrontations' I had intended should take me practically to the end of the play, began to write themselves at a terrific speed. Within three pages, I had dealt with the opening situation and felt I'd got to introduce some further action, so I brought in an extra character. Within five pages, the play was drawing to a close – and there was nothing at all I could do about it. In despair, I abandoned the opus and decided I'd never be able to write a play.

I mention this because if I had had the benefit of being able to read this book, I would not have made the task difficult for myself by making this first serious attempt at a one-act play a psychological drama of relationships, with a cast of three!

Later, I plunged into playwriting again with an involved story I have already mentioned, that of the pig with the wonderful operatic voice, and managed to get to the end successfully, because the play was filled with lots of incidents which kept it moving, it wasn't the least bit deep or psychological, and the cast list numbered 18 plus extras!

To point the moral here, I will add that after I had written quite a lot of plays, I revived the deep psychological drama and re-wrote it. This time, I had the experience of dialogue and characterisation, structure and form, to make it into a decent play without altering the story. I also managed to write it to the right length, purely because I had learned how to write plays properly. But the story was just the same, the twists and turns of the plot were no different. So if you find your play has written itself too soon, or you can't make it long enough, don't try to patch up the ending somehow, put your story on one side until you've had a few more attempts, and then come back to it. After all, if you were a music student, you wouldn't expect to create a sonata that would stand comparison with those of the great composers at your first attempt. It doesn't mean you can't write, and it doesn't mean you can't write a play. Give yourself a chance and don't expect miracles the first time you put pen to paper.

Although the climax might well be something different from what the audience was expecting, there are certain things you have to include in your play if you have introduced references to them, or else this will create another form of anticlimax. There are some scenes which obviously *must* be included or the whole effect is wrong and the audience will feel cheated and frustrated.

Say your play is based on the fact that identical twins are involved, and they keep creating havoc among the other characters by referring to 'my twin brother, George' or 'my twin brother Henry'. Implicit in speeches like: 'Oh, I'm not surprised you thought I was Henry – nobody could ever tell us apart', or 'No, I'm not Henry, I'm George', is the fact that at some stage, the twins must appear *together* and out of their joint appearance, will spring a great deal of further confusion which will then, since they are both there, proceed to sort itself out for good.

In the same way, if one of the characters is always referring to the fact that his wife is quite happy for him to have affairs with other women, the audience will expect something to come of this cryptic remark. They will be waiting for the scene where the wife actually *says* she doesn't mind about the affairs – and then takes the matter further by, perhaps, telling her unfaithful husband that she doesn't mind about the other women because she no longer cares about *him*, and is going to leave him for somebody else. Thus he becomes trapped by what had been a way of protecting himself against his own misdeeds. The tables get turned – somebody has cried 'Wolf!' once too often – the person who flattered himself he'd managed to escape his punishment has actually put the noose round his own neck.

If you have led up to any scene where the characters are anticipating events; preparing for the great moment; screwing their courage up to do something – then it is essential that (if possible) this scene should be viewed by the audience, not glossed over and left out. If, in the story of Cinderella, we are allowed to see the Fairy Godmother promising Cinders in her rags that she *will* go to the ball, we would feel cheated if we were not allowed to share in the splendour of her transformation into a radiant beauty who turns all heads as she is announced, sparklingly lovely in her wonderful ball gown, at the palace. How disappointed we would be if, after the Fairy Godmother has told her she is to go to the ball, the next scene was the arrival home of the Ugly Sisters, who were very put out at Cinders' impertinence and described how she had dared to dance with the Prince. How frustrating it would be if we never saw Cinders in her finery, but only in her rags again the next day!

So if you have promised your audience a 'big scene' in any way, make sure they get it, and don't cheat them of what they are looking forward to with more interest than the characters who will be involved in the action. Don't try to be too clever, to invent ways round the 'obvious' ending if this is going to disappoint the audience, or make them feel they had their treat snatched from their grasp at the last moment.

The last point about the climax of your play is to be aware that you must not leave the audience hanging, as it were, on the high point of your graph and ring down the curtain without giving them a gentle push towards less elevated ground. It will of course depend on your play, but generally, you never end on the actual climax itself, you give the audience at least a few moments of 'unwinding time' before you bring down the final curtain. Sometimes various characters may indulge in a sort of 'rounding off' or 'summing up' of the action. Shakespeare used this method quite a lot. The climax of *Romeo And Juliet* is, of course, the suicide of Juliet when she wakes from her drugged sleep and finds that her love, thinking she was really dead, has already taken poision. Once the lovers are dead, the play is over, but there is a 'winding-down' as the bodies are discovered, as explanations are made, as the feud between the Montagues and Capulets is declared over by the sorrowing families, and as the final speech summing up the events of the play is pronounced by Prince Escalus. It would have been most unsatisfactory for the audience if Shakespeare had constructed the play so that all the explanations were more or less finished with and the parents of the lovers had declared that if anything happened to their children, they would be so heart-broken that they'd end the feud for ever – and *then* showed us that dramatic climax in the vault where Romeo took the poison and Juliet, waking, stabbed herself with his dagger.

Generally, it is impossible to end on a note of high emotion. Explanations have to be given, however brief these may be – the various threads of the play have to be gathered together and neatly tied up so that the audience can feel there is no outstanding point which hasn't been satisfactorily dealt with.

Even if the play is a comedy and the climax is hilariously funny, you can't ring down the curtain as the players and the audience are at the point of collapse – the players from the contortions of the climax and the audience from hysterics. Neither can you ring down the curtain in the middle of a highly dramatic argument or verbal battle. Every situation has to work itself through to its natural ending, and the intensity of an emotional or dramatic (or even extremely funny) situation must be allowed to alter pitch and let the audience relax a bit before the curtain descends for the last time. Do not leave them dangling, as it were, in a state of highly charged involvement which is suddenly withdrawn from their grasp. Let them find their feet, see that life is going to go on for the characters in the play – even if there is only the slightest indication of this – and that the excitement is really over, before you cut them off from the world where they have been existing during the performance.

It does not really matter whether you, as the playwright, specify that there should be a SLOW CURTAIN or a QUICK CURTAIN at the end of your play, since the producer will alter this if he feels it doesn't fit in with his interpretation of your script. Generally, an amusing play can end more briskly than a tragic one. Slow endings, quiet endings, brooding endings, all of these would be more suited to a serious or a tragic play; quick endings, fast curtains on the last 'laugh' and the final comment of the dialogue – these would be better for farce, or funny plays.

Often, a play may end with a gesture rather than words being spoken. When the action is all over and one of the characters is left alone, for instance, they may think for a few seconds, then do something which signifies what their future attitude is going to be, or how the play has affected them. You might, for instance, have dealt with the problems of an alcoholic in your play, and at the end, he is left alone, his wife has left him, and all including his job, is lost. In the last few moments of the play, he sits moodily with his head in his hands once his wife has gone, then gets to his feet, stumbles to the table and pours out a drink from the bottle that stands on it. Then he lifts the glass to his lips, hesitates, puts it down again and rushes across to the phone. The wife, perhaps, has been pleading with him throughout the play to get help, to try and fight his drink problem and he has refused, blamed her, maintained that there is no problem to be overcome.

As he clutches the phone, shaking, he consults the Directory and begins to dial, glancing at the glass on the table as though terrified of it . . .

THE CURTAIN FALLS.

Chapter Nine

WHAT TYPE OF PLAY?

There are obviously great differences between comedy and tragedy, farce and melodrama, but if you have some idea of what those differences are, and why an audience will laugh at a farce, and feel sad at a tragedy, this will help you when you are wondering what will be the best treatment to give your own idea. For, though some plays have simply got to be funny while others are on very serious topics, you may be surprised to hear that quite often, the same plot could be either serious or funny, depending on the treatment.

Take the classic visual joke of the man slipping on a banana-skin. If we see a stranger in the street – particularly a rather pompous and officious-looking businessman – lose his dignity in this way, the effect might well be amusing. But if we happen to know the man, and we are aware that his wife is seriously ill in hospital, and the officious-looking stare is actually his way of trying to pretend he's not worrying, when really he's at his wits' end, we are more likely to be moved to pity and sympathy if we should see him stagger and lurch before sitting down abruptly.

It is the same with comedy and tragedy, to a certain extent. In farce, where the plot is usually highly improbable, and involves a desperate attempt to keep up appearances at all costs, the characters are simple stereotypes and are rarely deep or complex individuals. There are no memorable characters to haunt us after we have watched a farce. They may have names, but we are more likely to remember them as types – the harassed husband, the suspicious wife, the dumb blonde. If we – the audience – ever began to take the characters in a farce seriously, or worried about what Harry's wife would do if she did discover Gloria hiding in the bedroom, the playwright has failed. The play would stop being funny and become rather embarrassing. Serious problems and complicated explorations of the human condition are not intended to be present in a farce, and we accept this and find difficult situations amusing rather than upsetting, since, like the unknown man in the street slipping on the banana-skin, the characters are largely 'just people' to us, not – as we feel is the case with a character like Hamlet – intimate friends.

So if you are planning to write a farce, bear in mind that what will matter most will not be your wonderful characterization but the innumerable twists, turns and incidents of your plot and the fact that in farce, most the action centres on the efforts of practically every character to keep 'secrets' from the others. These secrets will usually be of an extra-marital sexual nature, and much of the comedy comes from the fact that in order to conceal their indiscretions and keep up appearances, the characters spend most of the play telling the most outrageous untruths. Blatant fabrications uttered by rather shallow characters are invariably amusing to an audience, and the more ridiculous the lie, the more the audience will laugh.

The visual element is also extremely important in farce, especially the 'bedroom farce', where the characters are generally driven to scurrying about in embarrassing states of undress, but remember that in a farce, it is not the undressing itself, or the loss of the hero's trousers, which provides the comedy, but the contrast between the respectability the characters are trying to maintain and their actual inability to keep these appearances up. Farce is more difficult to write than many people imagine.

In a comedy, the characters are not stereotypes, they have to be much more credible as people, and the plot too has to be plausible rather than the unbelievable antics of a farce. Mary and George in *A Fishy Business* are human beings with whom the audience can identify, a husband and wife who have their little running battles but who nevertheless support each other and present a united front to their guests to get their dinner party over successfully. The catastrophe with the salmon, the hasty substitution of tinned fish covered with greens which they serve to themselves – all this is the sort of thing that an audience would feel could easily happen to them if they had an Uncle Richard who'd presented them with a fresh salmon and they'd left it lying within reach of the cat in their efforts to get ready for their guests and create a good impression. Comedy reveals human failings and foibles, but in a sympathetic manner. The audience is laughing good-naturedly at itself, admitting ruefully that, yes, we're an odd lot really, aren't we, but since we're all in the same boat, why not enjoy the fact that we're all human and that we all muddle through as best we can?

Almost any subject can be treated in an amusing manner. Practically nothing is sacred. Take the theme of death, for instance. You might think that a play about death would have to be a tragedy – or a serious drama, at the very least – but there are many successful examples of hilarious plays about death, the most well-known possibly being Joseph Kesselring's *Arsenic And Old Lace*, where the sweet harmless elderly ladies who are the heroines turn out to be mass-murderers and their nephew a homicidal maniac. The same theme – though this was a film not a play – brought the comedy to *Kind Hearts And Coronets*, where the members of an aristocratic family are disposed of one by one so that the murderer can inherit a dukedom.

You might choose to write a comedy about a lady who became madly infatuated with the local undertaker (though this is not a new idea), and who could only manage to contrive to keep meeting him by killing off all the members of her family in turn so that he'd have to keep visiting her in his official capacity.

I would just like to point out here that if you are of an extremely serious nature, and don't have much of a sense of humour (a matter which need never be made public!) it is not very likely that you are going to be able to write a comedy with any great degree of success, so you would do better not to try. Nobody can be taught to write in an amusing or funny manner; wit, humour, a flair for farce or the ridiculous are integral parts of some people's make-up, which are just not there in the personalities of others, and no matter how hard someone who has no real gift for humour might try to make his or her play funny, the effect will only be embarrassingly forced and contrived. You can't *learn* humour. It is either there or it isn't – and if it isn't, don't worry, that's nothing to be ashamed of. Ibsen was not specially gifted with a talent for humour, but his plays are no less great because of that.

Inexperienced playwrights often come to grief because they are unaware of the delicate difference between drama and what we would call melodrama, though melodramas as such are no longer a popular form of writing, as they were during the Victorian era.

Melodrama then meant not just a strongly dramatic play, but one which employed all the resources of the theatre to bombard the audience with extreme and sensational situations calling for wildly exaggerated emotion from the players. Melodramas then held audiences spell-bound; now we regard 'melodramatics' as rather silly, and producers will want to avoid at all costs any form of 'hamming' or 'over-acting' in a production, because they know that however serious the play, exaggerated emotion, hand-wringings, staggerings and facial contortions of agony as the cast wallow in melodrama, will these days be certain to make an audience laugh.

So playwrights who think they are writing serious drama but have not yet learned not to go 'over the top' can often write in a melodramatic manner in their enthusiasm to make an impact. Does the following example sound something like the style of your elevated new play? If so, beware, for this is melodramatic writing:

> MARIE: (hesitantly) Robert – Robert, darling –
> ROBERT: (without looking at her) You! I thought I told you to leave and never come back.
> MARIE: I – I couldn't. Robert, I know I've hurt you – wounded you – but I'd do anything to wipe out these last few weeks now. I didn't realise it, but in hurting you, I was hurting myself even more. I can't bear the thought of your pain – I'd rather suffer double the agony myself – Oh, Robert, can you bring yourself to forgive me? – to take me back?
> ROBERT: How can you ask that? I worshipped you – I adored you, and you flung everything back in my face when you – (he breaks down)
> MARIE: (driven) I never betrayed you, Robert, I swear. Oh, I know it seemed like that – and even now, I can't explain why I had to behave as I did – (aside) Oh, God, what can I say to convince him that it's he, my husband, whom I've loved all along? That it was only to save Frederick that I agreed to the deception?
> ROBERT: (harshly) Go, before I forget that I loved you and take it upon myself to rid the world of a – a murderess!
> MARIE: (holding out her hands) Robert, I beg you – !
> ROBERT: Go, I say!

(MARIE stumbles out, weeping heart-brokenly)

It is in melodrama that such tricks as the 'aside' are used.

Characters in a play today may mutter beneath their breath, but it will not be the same sort of thing that the melodramatic 'aside' consisted of. In melodrama, the 'aside' was generally some sort of comment to the audience, who could supposedly hear the comment while the other characters on the stage could not. Remarks like: 'I dare not let him suspect!' or 'Can he have guessed the truth?' are typical 'asides'. In melodrama too, monologues where characters talked to themselves about the way events were shaping up were often included, with no attempt to make them seem like realistic dialogue. Thus the murderer-to-be of the ill-fated Maria Marten might have mused, as he dug a grave ready for her body at the Red Barn:

'The very heavens seem to cry out a warning tonight. Will she come, I wonder? Will she dare the dark and the storm? Her last journey to the grave! Yes, fool as she is, she'll make that journey, for she loves me, and she would dare anything for my sake, the sake of the father of her child. Ah – a light flickers across the field! Tis Maria – ! Lighting her way to her death!'

It is worth pointing out here that even in the most realistic modern play, characters may, because of the fact that the scene is restricted to one set, have to hold a 'private' conversation. Two of them might talk down-stage while other activity is going on behind them, and they will obviously have to speak up so that the audience can hear what they are saying, but the playwright will have to give the impression that their words cannot be heard by the other characters in the same room, or whatever the setting is. An audience will accept that they can hear what other characters cannot, and you can get away with a great deal of this if required, but try to avoid the type of melodramatic 'aside' and monologue which will spoil the effect of natural-sounding dialogue.

Since the melodrama as a genre was at its most popular during the Nineteenth Century, most melodramas have stories set in the Victorian period. That of *Maria Marten* was based on an actual murder which took place in the 1820s, and another well-known subject was the plot of Mary Elizabeth Braddon's book *Lady Audley's Secret*, which has been dramatised several times. Most of the original Victorian melodramas have been lost, or were the rather uninspired work of unknown authors, but if you feel this is the sort of play you'd really like to get your teeth into, amateur companies do sometimes like to present a typical Victorian-type melodrama, where they might ask the audience to attend in suitable Victorian dress, and make an occasion of the production. It can be fun for everyone concerned, and this could include you as the playwright.

Serious-minded people might well feel that the straight drama is for them, but I would like to emphasise that a fully-fledged tragedy is difficult for a beginner, since the rules for tragic plays are different from the ones I have outlined in this book. A serious drama can work by the methods I have indicated, the posing of the Question, the resolution at the end, the feeling that, though sad, this is the rightful ending for the play.

A tragedy, however, of the same type as *Oedipus Rex* (the work of Sophocles) does not exactly pose a Question, but presents a tragic hero – who needs to have certain qualities in his character – in a position where doom is inevitable, and however the hero might try to escape his fate, it is impossible for him to do so. In a way, a tragedy is a sort of ritual through which both the players and the audience pass to emerge uplifted at the end by the catharsis of the experience. Though we may weep at the end of a deeply moving tragedy, the tears are healing, and there is a sort of exultation in them. According to Aristotle, tragedy purifies or eliminates temporarily from our system various destructive elements, and so makes us feel better rather than worse, more at peace with ourselves and everyone else.

Thus a tragedy is concerned with the inevitability of doom and the way in which this doom will come, rather than an inter-action between the characters leading to certain happenings that carry the plot forward. In a tragedy, the plot has already been pre-destined, and the events which will take place laid down. If you feel this type of writing is for you, then study the Greek tragedies and the various commentaries which are available on Greek drama and you may find that the discipline of having to fit your work into very strict rules will be a positive inspiration rather than a difficult chore.

The tragedies of Shakespeare are not constructed in the same way as the Greek tragedies. There is more of a possibility that the tragic hero – Macbeth, Othello, Hamlet – might stand a chance of escaping from the doom that awaits him but that due to a certain twist of his own personality, he is fated to go towards that doom, even though, if he had been a different sort of character, he might have chosen to take an entirely different course. The characters of the protagonists are more important in Elizabethan tragedy than in those of the Greek writers, and here again, if you feel this subject is the sort of thing you'd like to tackle, study the relevant plays and the many scholarly works that are available about them.

I must add that there are certain types of plays where the audience is fully aware that the hero or heroine – like Mary, Queen of Scots, for instance – is going to meet a sad end. History cannot be altered. Mary has to go to her doom at Fotheringay; Katheryn Howard will die, her head on the block as the executioner's sword sweeps down. So if you write a play about a historical person who did meet a tragic fate, you cannot pretend it didn't happen, and possibly it will be all the more moving for your audience if there is some foreshadowing of the doom that has got to come.

But you do not have to write tragically about such characters. You may choose to deal with a hopeful incident in the life of Mary of Scotland – your play might be a pointing of the fact that it was her son, the little Prince James, who eventually brought England and Scotland beneath one rule and healed the breaches between the two countries, for instance. Characters like Anne Boleyn do not have to move in doom-laden solemnity through a play, just because we know they came to a sad end. But it is as well to bear in mind, even in the happiest moments of plays dealing with historical figures who met some sort of tragic fate, that the knowledge that their doom must inevitably come will be at the back of the audience's mind all the time, making the portrayal of their eagerness to live all the more poignant.

My last word about different types of plays is that it is often impossible to categorise plays. As I have said, a serious play may have moments so amusing that they are what we remember when the play is over; or a comedy may contain moments of deep sadness. So do not try too hard to fit your play into any particular category beyond following the style and mood you need to craft it well and the rules which will make it a good play. That's all you really need to worry about.

Chapter Ten

INFORMATION

And when you have written your play, what then?

After performance might come, if you are lucky, a published version. The largest publisher of plays for the amateur stage in this country – if not in the world – is Samuel French Ltd., and if you wish to try your luck with them, you will find them at:

Samuel French Ltd.,
52 Fitzroy Street,
London W1P 6JR

They are always willing to consider scripts for publication, and if you have followed the basic rules set out in this book for the lay-out of your script, they will find this perfectly readable.

They prefer the completed play rather than just an idea, and it is helpful if your work has had at least a rehearsed reading, if not actual production, as this indicates that the script is workable on a stage.

To keep up with the sort of plays that are currently being published, you can ask to be put on French's Mailing List free of charge, though obviously, if you want to buy any scripts or Catalogues of Plays, you will have to pay for these. They also put out a certain amount of information on the Mailing List about what other publishers are doing in the field of drama, so if you want to start building up a picture of the state of playwriting, plays, what's happening at the moment, or a general picture of the market, Samuel French will be a good place to lead off.

Another publisher of plays for amateurs is:

New Playwrights' Network,
35 Sandringham Road,
Macclesfield,
Cheshire
SK10 1QB

This firm does, however, charge a reading fee, so before you submit a play, it would be wise to enquire about the amount. Even if your play is rejected, you will receive a report from their experienced readers which might help you to see what was wrong so that you won't make the same mistake again.

Other publishers of drama and useful addresses can be found in the 'Writers' and Artists' Year Book', which you can consult at your local library if you don't want to go to the expense of buying a copy, but most publishers apart from the two I have mentioned don't deal in plays for amateurs.

A treasure-house of information about playwriting, plays and the theatre exists at the home of the British Theatre Association (formerly the Drama League). This is at:

The British Theatre Association,
Cranbourn Mansions,
Cranbourn Street,
London WC2H 7AG

The BTA can answer any questions or queries that are bothering you, and if you are in London, you can consult its Play Library, which contains 56,000 titles, as well as its immense Reference Library facilities. If you want to get the full benefit of the faciltiies the BTA offers its members on

114

all aspects of theatre, the fee to join is £25 per year for individual membership, and this means you will get discounts not only on theatre tickets but on all courses and classes run by the BTA, which include tuition in playwriting. There is also an assessment and criticism service which can give you help and advice with your plays for a modest fee. Further details about the other benefits of membership can be obtained from the Association at their address above.

You can enquire at your local Arts Association about opportunities for playwrights, grants, or any courses on playwriting. Your local Council will probably have the details of Drama Festivals where there may be competitions for original plays, and often details of such events are available in local libraries. Another opportunity for drama (though not for the stage) is in the competitions that are run by local radio stations for radio plays. Keep your eyes and ears open for details of anything like this if you want to carry on with your playwriting.

The Arvon Foundation organises two extremely good series of courses on various aspects of writing – including drama. The addresses are:

The Arvon Foundation,
Lumb Bank,
Hebden Bridge,
West Yorks
HX7 6DF.

The Arvon Foundation,
Totleigh Barton,
Sheepwash,
Devon
EX21 5NS

Details of the course, tutors and so on are available from these addresses.

And in general, if you want to keep in touch with amateur theatre, have an idea of what is going on, what sort of plays are being performed, events and so on, the best way to do this is to order AMATEUR STAGE magazine from your newsagent. This is the only publication that deals with the amateur stage, and it is full of information about what all the amateur societies are performing, what new plays and new theatre books are coming out, anything that will interest amateurs.

There is a very active amateur theatre in this country, and most societies are only too pleased to take advantage of a new playwright, especially if he or she seems to know what he's doing. So, having got your first play (we hope) under your belt, keep reading and studying the ways other people have gained their effects on the stage, keep learning your craft, keep gaining experience at writing and also at seeing how your work translates into the three-dimensional medium when it is being performed. A whole new world could be waiting for you.

As they say in the theatre: Break a leg!

Translated, that means: I wish you the best of luck!

Plays by Dilys Gater:

FUGITIVE LIKE THE WIND (French)
THE SINGING SWANS (New Playwrights' Network)
TURNABOUT (New Playwrights' Network)
THE CAVERN (New Playwrights' Network)
MIRAGE (New Playwrights' Network)
HEAVEN FORBID! (New Playwrights' Network)
THE DAY BEFORE (New Playwrights' Network)

Writing as Dilys Owen:

PERCIVAL, THE PERFORMING PIG (French)
CAROLINE COMES FOR TEA (French)

PLAY-GAMES (Muller, 1977)